Praise for the First Edition of *Gender: Your Guide*

"This guide is a must-have for everyone, and not only those who are trans, gender nonconforming, or nonbinary—or who have someone trans in their life. Airton is speaking to a larger challenge in the culture: what Airton calls 'gender unfriendliness.' What I like most about how the author writes is how they combine their knowledge about gender, language, and identity with a warm and caring tone. I feel like Airton is both my smartest and best friend on this subject matter. And for anyone who finds themselves confused by the new acronyms and categories of sexual identity, the glossary alone is worth the price of this book."

—STEVEN PETROW,
The Washington Post

"I wish I had a copy of this book to give to every teacher, principal, counsellor, parent, partner, boss, and coworker of a trans, gender-variant, or nonbinary person in the world. I sincerely do. This book is for anyone who wants to learn and do better by trans and nonbinary people. Thoughtfully and compassionately written by someone who has lived experience of navigating the binary world in a nonbinary body and mind, Dr. Lee Airton will talk you through it all without pretense or judgment. It's not just a how-to guide to pronouns, gender-neutral language, and dismantling our very cisgendered systems, it is something so much more valuable: It's a why-should-we-all guide to building a more accessible and just world for people of all genders."

—IVAN COYOTE,
author of *Tomboy Survival Guide* and *Gender Failure*

Praise for the First Edition of *Gender: Your Guide*

"This is an invaluable resource for both new and veteran allies, especially with Airton's empathetic approach, which regularly acknowledges and validates challenges. Despite the brevity of the work, the author packs an incredible amount of information and advice into clear and succinct prose. General readers and scholars alike will benefit from the 'gender-friendly tool kit' and Airton's straightforward explanations and advice. VERDICT: This guide is unlike anything else available today, and an obvious and necessary item for collections of all kinds."

—ABBY HARGREAVES,
Library Journal (starred review)

"Today's workplaces must reflect the reality that gender is not as simple as previously thought. Understanding how to include everyone, regardless of how they identify and express their gender, is the key to unlocking the potential of any workforce. *Gender: Your Guide* provides the tools necessary for employers of any size to respond to the changing needs of employees and job seekers."

—COLIN DRUHAN,
executive director of Pride at Work Canada

"Dr. Airton is the perfect brilliant-but-accessible, frank-but-kind guide to our current LGBTQ language and landscape. *Gender: Your Guide* is without a doubt the most delightful and focused road map I've seen to treating trans people (and yourself!) with dignity."

—JEFFREY MARSH,
nonbinary activist and author of *How to Be You:
Stop Trying to Be Someone Else and Start Living Your Life*

GENDER:

The Gender-Friendly Primer on

YOUR

What to Know, What to Say, and

2ND EDITION

GUIDE

What to Do in the New Gender Culture

Lee Airton, PhD

ADAMS MEDIA
New York   London   Toronto   Sydney   New Delhi

Adams Media
An Imprint of Simon & Schuster, LLC
100 Technology Center Drive
Stoughton, Massachusetts 02072

This Adams Media trade paperback edition June 2024
First Adams Media hardcover edition October 2018

ADAMS MEDIA and colophon are registered trademarks of Simon & Schuster, LLC.

Simon & Schuster: Celebrating 100 Years of Publishing in 2024

For information about special discounts for bulk purchases, please contact Simon & Schuster Special Sales at 1-866-506-1949 or business@simonandschuster.com.

The Simon & Schuster Speakers Bureau can bring authors to your live event. For more information or to book an event, contact the Simon & Schuster Speakers Bureau at 1-866-248-3049 or visit our website at www.simonspeakers.com.

Interior design by Colleen Cunningham
Interior image © 123RF/Anna Kudinova

Manufactured in the United States of America

1 2024

Library of Congress Cataloging-in-Publication Data
Names: Airton, Lee, author.
Title: Gender: your guide, 2nd edition / Lee Airton, PhD.
Description: 2nd edition. | Stoughton, Massachusetts: Adams Media, 2024. | Includes bibliographical references and index.
Identifiers: LCCN 2023049263 | ISBN 9781507220313 (pb) | ISBN 9781507220320 (ebook)
Subjects: LCSH: Gender identity. | Parenting. | Parent and child.
Classification: LCC HQ1075 .A3577 2024 | DDC 305.3--dc23/eng/20231102
LC record available at https://lccn.loc.gov/2023049263

ISBN 978-1-5072-2031-3
ISBN 978-1-5072-2032-0 (ebook)

In loving memory of Granville Airton (1942–2022),
my Dear Old Dad, who endlessly loved his
nonbinary kid without needing to understand
every single thing. Dad was proud to have
contributed everyone's favorite thing in the book:
"There they are—Person America!"

Contents

Part Two.
WHAT TO SAY
101

Part Three.
WHAT TO DO
163

Acknowledgments

Since the first edition was published, thank you to everyone who hosted me for talks, fireside chats, and book club meetings. I have a special place in my heart for educators who read the book and chatted with me about its connections to your work. Thank you to those who let me know the book helped you to have necessary and tender conversations with people you love. This is why I wrote it, and you have brought the book to life.

This book exists because people have shared with me, in my capacities as a blogger, educator, researcher, colleague, friend, partner, and community member. I do not believe that knowledge is a single-author proposition. I am particularly grateful for expertise shared by Ali Greey, Lex Konnelly, Bronwyn Bjorkman, Kyle Kirkup, and Anthony Michael Kreis. May this book honor the relationships that gave it life and that have given me the means and capacity to do my work.

I acknowledge all of the transgender-spectrum people before and alongside me who have participated in knowledge creation about gender from our unique yet multiplicitous perspectives. I acknowledge the work of others who seek ways to make gender more joyful and less harmful. My bibliography is a testament to just how much work has been done that informs my own.

At Adams Media, I acknowledge Laura Daly, Colleen Mulhern, Annie Franklin, and the press for postponing the second edition when my dad suddenly died. I also thank my agent Samantha Haywood and others at the Transatlantic Agency.

I acknowledge the many cisgender people who have shared with me their experiences of gender's rigid expectations. Some of their stories are in this book, and I offer gratitude to my sister and champion, Megan Airton Cindric, and my friend and teacher, the late Brianna O'Connor Hersey.

My local queer and trans community in Kingston, Ontario, and my colleagues and students across Queen's University continue to sustain me and teach me. My local public school board, Limestone DSB, works hard to welcome all the ways kids experience gender, and I acknowledge Suchetan James, Laura Gillam, Ellyn Clost-Lambert, Rae McDonald, Andrea Barrow, Patty Gollogly, and all the other good people making it possible for trans and gender-nonconforming kids to "see themselves in Limestone." I also acknowledge the Second Heart and Kingston sanghas.

To my home team: Wilding, Berard, Crystal, Dre, Megan, and Zach. Thank you for taking good care of me, of Tama, and of each other. I am grateful for each of you in my corner as (most of us) begin the second half of our lives.

Thirteen years on, and through all the changes, I still get to spend every day with the person who knows me best of all: Dr. Tamara de Szegheo Lang. Thank you for honoring me with parts of yourself nobody else sees, even if that means you're a huge brat. I am excited to be old people together.

Lastly, I lift up the memory of former Adams Media acquisitions editor Cate Coulacos Prato and send my love to her husband and son. Cate was the one who saw the need for a book like this in the world, found me blogging away in relative obscurity at TheyIsMy Pronoun.com, and made *Gender: Your Guide* happen.

Preface: Why This Book Matters

Big reveal: When I'm in an airport, I usually have to go to the bathroom. No big deal, right? Airports have lots of bathrooms.

Well, visiting a gendered bathroom actually *is* a big deal for me. Many airports still don't have gender-neutral bathrooms, or enough of them, so I'm forced to choose one side or the other. Waiting for the plane, where every bathroom is blessedly gender-neutral, isn't always possible. Decision made, I take a breath and begin my approach to the women's. (Why the women's? Having seen bathrooms of all kinds in my time, the women's is reliably clean and there is no urinal cake. These are the only reasons.)

Entering the area outside any bathroom that splits into men's and women's facilities is like going onstage. I could give someone detailed directions on how to handle it. I'm aware of my clothing; often when I'm traveling for business, this means a blazer, a crispy button-down, and dark jeans. I'm aware of the speed of my walk, of when to stop meandering and begin a more purposeful stride. Sometimes I head toward a water fountain between the entrances: a gender time-out. If anyone is watching me, they're likely appeased by this neutral destination and move along, in search of other distractions. Once at the water fountain, I can slip inside the bathroom door.

When I enter the women's bathroom, I puff out my chest as much as I can and begin clearing my throat in an artificially high register. Sometimes I hum loud and high like Fräulein Maria traversing the Alps. I smile maniacally and make inviting eye contact with anyone I meet at the threshold or inside to show that I come in peace and I am confident that this is the correct washroom for me despite appearances (it isn't, but when you have to go, you have to go). I choose the first stall I see even though the first stall isn't usually one's first choice. I enter, I lock the door, I sit down, I breathe. If the bathroom is busy, I might linger a little while in private, feeling the muscles around my eyes, mouth, and shoulders relax.

I make a mistake every time, though. Having put friendly Fräulein Maria back on for the handwashing experience, I relax and let it all go as I exit. This is where it always happens.

One time as I was exiting the women's bathroom in the airport, a woman was fast approaching the two entrances while speaking on the phone. Seeing me exiting one of the bathrooms, she automatically adjusted course. She strode right into the men's bathroom before realizing where she was. And screamed!

• • •

This kind of thing has been happening to me for a very long time. Bathrooms are unavoidable places in everyday life where gender is intensified and where people's bodies are scrutinized to determine who belongs and who doesn't. Among transgender (or trans) people—those like me whose gender identity doesn't align easily or at all with the M or F we were assigned at birth—bathroom stories are a genre that verges on cliché. You do all you can to pass (to be read like the symbol on the bathroom sign), you get clocked (recognized as transgender), and you get out of there as fast as possible.

My bathroom story walked you through the energy-intensive process I go through to do something that most people do without thinking at all. For many trans people, using the bathroom requires thought, planning, and constant vigilance. Other ordinary things take more energy as well, like shopping for clothes that both fit my body and help others to see who I am. I've acquired the necessary skills to get by in these situations from years of learning and practice, and because older or more experienced transgender people have taken the time to teach and support me. The thinking, planning, teaching, and learning can add up to a marathon every time I head outside, even when all I need is a bag of chips or a bag of milk (a thing in Canada). That's one reason why this book is necessary.

I started with a bathroom story so that I could clear up a common misconception about why transgender people need you, the person who picked up this book: that the thing transgender people experience when others get our gender wrong is offense, or that we are offended. I often hear people say that they're scared of "offending" transgender people or that causing offense is the bad thing they want to avoid. This can be a source of tremendous anxiety, and it can make someone go out of their way to avoid a trans person just for fear of offending them. But trans people have far worse experiences than being offended, like being assaulted. In between being offended and being assaulted, there is a whole range of reasons why transgender people need others to get into the work of changing how gender works, for and alongside us. Many of these reasons have to do with the everyday exhaustion of being who we are, not being offended.

Trans people can avoid the bathroom sometimes, but we can't avoid other people and the language we use to communicate with each other. For many trans people, everyday communication and interaction are situations where our well-being and mental health are actively, gradually either beefed up or run down—often by people around us who may have no idea how their words or actions affect our capacity to participate in the world. I'm not talking about those people who are set on doing us harm or denying our existence, but people who just haven't had to think about how gender rigidly structures our lives, spaces, and interactions.

And so, when someone accidentally misgenders me—applies an incorrect gender pronoun, term, or title—I'm not offended. There's no surge of righteous indignation. It's less of a filling-up with feelings and more of an emptying-out of energy. After a day of continuous misgendering, I feel like the balloon you find under the couch a week after the festivities: deflated. I'm sometimes too tired to correct or educate even the kindest and most understanding person in the world—too tired to be kind or understanding in turn, and too tired to be the best person I can be.

In the years since I came out as transgender, I've also noticed something wonderful: the incredible effect of people getting things right. When people use or infer my correct pronouns, or use terms for me that match my gender identity, they make an incredible, palpable difference to my well-being. These seemingly small and ordinary things fill up my gas tank. Lee on a full tank is a kinder, gentler person who isn't always on guard against the gendered expectations buried in so much of our everyday lives and language. And when I don't have to expend my extra energy on correcting, explaining, and self-advocating, I'm also more likely to choose fresh air, the gym, or a friend date over Netflix and couch. Moreover, I'm a better listener, teacher, coworker, partner, sibling, kid, untie (a gender-neutral alternative to aunt or uncle), friend, and even stranger. All this is to say that every ounce of transgender knowledge, skill, and energy will not make everyday life more welcoming for transgender people if we're the only ones making an effort. It takes too great a toll on transgender people to do all of the correcting, explaining, and advocating required to make gender less exhausting all around.

This is where you come in, and that's why I wrote this book. In fact, I imagine you picked up my book specifically because you want to get involved in the work of creating a more gender-friendly world around you. I'm very glad you did because we need you. Perhaps you already know a gaggle of trans people, or perhaps you've never (knowingly) met one of us. You might have picked up this book because you want to better understand and support your trans or gender-nonconforming sibling, parent, or child. Or you might want to be ready for the next time you meet someone whose pronouns you aren't sure about. Or you might be well aware of how rigid gender rules and expectations have made your own life more difficult than it needs to be. For any and all of these reasons, this book is for you. I study gender diversity in education and can share what is known about transgender people's experiences through research. But I'm also a transgender person myself—a nonbinary one at that (which I'll come back to in Chapter 3)—who has been involved in trans communities for many years. In 2011, I changed my name and changed my pronoun to singular *they*. I have a master's and a PhD in education, and realized that the world was missing an educational resource, whether for me, for other gender-neutral pronoun users, or for the people in our lives who have to talk about us all the time, because life. And so, I founded *They Is My Pronoun* in 2012: the first Q+A blog on gender-neutral pronoun usage and user support, archived in 2020.

The experience of running my blog and traveling around to speak about gender-neutral pronouns and diversity under the "T" has brought me into conversation with many people who are working hard to have their gender needs met and to meet the needs of others. For over fifteen years, I've taught in teacher education programs and engaged hundreds of preservice teachers in learning about their professional responsibility toward all of their students and all of the ways they do gender, whether they are under the transgender umbrella or not. I've also learned a great deal about the wealth of gendered experience and expertise that we all bring into our interactions with others but don't think about as a resource.

What I have learned from all of this teaching, learning, and just living life as a nonbinary transgender person is as follows: I am more interested in people being able to live gender in diverse ways with happiness than in forcible conformity in the service of a rigid two-category system. I am more interested in recognizing the gender possibilities that are already here than in denying that these possibilities have been here since before history began to be written (and regardless, because not all history is written). I am equally interested in the gender happiness of transgender people and nontransgender people. For these reasons, I'm committed to helping gender do its work with fewer expectations and less harm. This is the approach that I bring to this book.

Introduction

Gender is changing. It seems like more and more people aren't doing gender in the usual way. More people than ever before—children, youth, and adults—are coming out and openly living their lives as transgender men or women. Whether transgender or not, many young people are expressing gender in ways that don't line up with traditional expectations. A growing number of transgender people are using gender-neutral titles like Mx. and personal pronouns like singular *they*. Definitive style manuals like *The Associated Press Stylebook* and *The Chicago Manual of Style*, as well as major newspapers like *The Washington Post*, have included singular *they* in their guidelines for years now. And while varying widely in wording and scope, according to an article by Kyle Kirkup in the *University of Toronto Law Journal*, there are legal protections for gender diversity in every Canadian province and territory, in thirty-three American states, and in the District of Columbia.

Some people feel like these changes threaten traditional ways of living, and are even putting children and youth at risk. Since the first edition of this book was published in 2018, these views have emerged into daylight and even legislation in the US, as well as Canadian mainstream media. This second edition has been fully updated to directly address this particular moment in time: when doing your best to make gender-friendly changes may get you caught up in larger conversations. That said, many people continue to recognize that gender diversity has always been with us and is only now coming out or even back into public life. No matter where you stand right now, it's clear that navigating this changing world of gender means ongoing shifts in our language and our everyday practices because gender is *everywhere*: in how we speak, write, move around in public space, and relate to one another.

Gender: Your Guide, 2nd Edition is a manual for making this shift yourself so that you can welcome all of the ways that people do gender, instead of calling others into question without even knowing it. I will teach you *how* to implement gender-friendly language and practices in your family and friendships, at work, and with people you meet every day. Beyond logistics, I'll also help you understand *why* it will benefit you to participate in welcoming the changing world of gender, because gender-friendliness is a good thing for *everyone*, not only people who are transgender. You'll come away from this fully updated second edition with all of the information you need to participate in creating a more gender-friendly world around you. This includes all new sections on trans kids, the phenomenon of "detransition," what it means when someone has *they/she* or *he/they* pronouns, and something so boring but so important: making things like registration forms inclusive of everyone. You will also find a brand-new set of common arguments against gender-friendly change in Chapter 9, including "It's unfair for trans girls/women to play sports!" (spoiler alert: it isn't), and learn how to speak back to each one using the latest research, common sense, and empathy.

There are also new stories in the second edition. In addition to those already in the book, I illustrate the importance of medical transition for many trans people by talking about my own decision to have top surgery in 2021. I also share more about my dad, who died unexpectedly in 2022, particularly how his approach to supporting me—loving over fully understanding—is something I wish for others too.

I hope that by reading this book and trying on my suggestions, you'll feel confident—if only more than you feel now—in working to make your world safer, nicer, and less exhausting for people who live gender in ways that weren't expected of us when we were born. This world can be your own home or the nexus of your extended family. It can be your workplace, church, mosque, choir, or disc golf team. The world you set your sights on changing can be your gym, the supermarket, or the bus. It can be anywhere you demonstrate a respect for everyone's self-determination in how they present and articulate their gender, and a willingness to do your best and make better mistakes in the process (because you will make them, and that's okay). It is anywhere you show others, whether transgender or not, that they are real, they are respected, and they are not out of place.

I've also included a special coda addressed "To the Trans Person Whose Person Is Reading This Book." I imagine interested non-transgender people will pick up *Gender: Your Guide, 2nd Edition*, but transgender people might also give it to others as a resource. The coda shares some self-advocacy strategies for transgender people based on what I've learned from many years of supporting and speaking with others about trying to get our gender-related needs met. But I also make an ask: that transgender people, to the best of our ability, understand that meeting our needs does take effort and is a process of learning and unlearning for the people around us. Being gender friendly is a process for all of us, and we're all at different places in this journey. *Gender: Your Guide, 2nd Edition* invites everyone to get on board to make gender more flexible and less constricting: a source of more joy, and less harm, for everyone. Let's get started.

PART ONE.

WHAT TO KNOW

In this part I will describe how gender works as an ongoing process that we all participate in. Each of us is a gender expert, which means that we know how to follow the rules of our gender category, as best as we can. These rules change depending on where we are, and our gender expertise is honed as we move among all the different places where we spend time, making changes in our gender expression—how we act, style, talk, groom, and present ourselves—as we go. You know how to do this deep down in your gut, even if you don't know that you know, and even if you haven't thought of yourself as a gender expert. We most often use our gender expertise to avoid standing out and getting called into question by others, which can be harmful. But we can put our expertise to use instead to create spaces where standing out doesn't mean getting called into question and doesn't have harmful consequences. In such spaces the "rules" are less like a set menu and more like a buffet: Take what you like, and leave the rest for others to enjoy.

You'll also learn about some people under the transgender umbrella. Like everyone else, transgender people were assigned a sex and corresponding gender category at birth, but this assignment doesn't reflect who we are. Transgender and cisgender people all work the same gender system—standing out and blending in, getting called into question and calling others into question too—but standing out can have worse consequences for transgender people. I debunk a common misconception that all trans people are on what I call a "binary" pathway, or moving from one side of the M-to-F binary to the other, and I will introduce three sometimes-overlapping groups of people under the "T": transgender people who are women or men, nonbinary transgender people who are neither, and people who are gender-fluid. You will learn that there's no one way to be in any of these groups, and that trans people face different challenges and have different relationships to being visible or out as transgender. I'll end Chapter 3 by explaining the concept of transition in a way that makes it clear that transition, like transgender, is a spectrum.

1.

Understanding Gender in Today's World

Fact or Process? Two Broad Schools of Thought about Gender

Biology and Socialization Affect Each Other

How Gender Works in Everyday Life

In this chapter I explain how gender works and how we all participate in its work. I begin with a broad-brush look at the two major schools of thought about gender and its relationship to biological sex: gender as a fact and gender as a process. A key distinction between these schools, both inside and outside of academic disciplines, is whether gender differences are attributed to biology or to how we are socialized by other people around us beginning at birth. Next I explain how gender works from the perspective of gender as an ongoing, lifelong process. We participate in this process every day of our lives, including visually and verbally, by calling others into question when they stand out. I explain many ways in which the question-calling happens, whether or not we know we're doing it. Thinking of gender as a process can help you begin seeing the role that gender plays and has played in your own life, from childhood. We also all have our own gender expertise, no matter our gender identity or gender expression. Naming yours is an important tool for creating a gender-friendly world around you.

It can be difficult to start making your own context more gender friendly if you don't have a sense of your starting place. And so, the end of this chapter gives you some tools to explore how gender currently plays out in spaces where you spend time. I call this process *drawing* your gender-friendly road map. I lead you through a reflection exercise where you'll use your own gender expertise to identify what someone might face in your family, community, friend group, or workplace if they bump up against others' gendered expectations. This will help you think and act proactively, as well as help you notice how gender might be restrictive there already.

Fact or Process? Two Broad Schools of Thought about Gender

We don't usually think of gender as something that *works*—a process, like housecleaning—but as something that just *is*: a fact, like whether the house is clean or dirty. Facts seem like dependable things that stand still, whereas processes seem like things that are on their way to standing still: to being facts. But many facts are actually processes in disguise.

I'll share an example of fact versus process that has nothing to do with gender and everything to do with a questionable life choice: living with two ginormous cats even though I have a cat allergy. Before the house is fully clean, my cats have already begun redistributing their fur and dander. My house is never "clean" or "dirty" (fact) because the cleaning is never complete (process). What's worse, the cats' redistribution of fur and dander is actually helped by running all over the house to escape the vacuum! The process is never complete. In the same way, we can think about gender as a process a person participates in that is never complete, and not something a person "just is."

Some people argue that gender is a fact about a person that we can know from birth and that it's basically the same thing as sex. People in this camp primarily attribute gender differences to biological sex differences, as opposed to the differences reinforced or even produced through society's expectations. Some in this camp even object to the term "gender" at all, claiming to reject "gender ideology" in favor of "sex-based rights" that they feel are infringed on by transgender people. In recent years, these views have come to prominence due in part to tweets by celebrated author J.K. Rowling. Rowling's initial viral tweet in 2020 expressed her skepticism at the phrase "people who menstruate." Why not just say "women," she argued, as it means the very same thing? This feels like common sense to many, and Rowling has become an accessible spokesperson for "gender is a fact" views. But these views tend to simplify very complex issues, like whether menstruation is necessary for womanhood. Even if someone denies that a person without a uterus can be a woman, they likely accept the fact that not every woman menstruates.

For those who are more in the "gender is a process" camp, being a woman or a man is more than a biological fact, like whether one menstruates or not. Rather, they believe that gender is a teaching and learning process that's never complete. In this camp gender differences are primarily attributed to socialization, including how we are socialized in relation to biology: what our bodies do (or do not do).

To better understand the two major schools of thought about gender—gender is a fact or gender is a process—let's think about the moment a baby is born. (Let's assume that the baby's parents have not been given information about the baby's body from an ultrasound in advance of the big day.) In a great tide of fluid and relief, the baby emerges. Someone (doctor, nurse, or midwife) catches the baby and notes the shape and size of their external genitalia. What happens next is largely based on the visual appearance of the genitalia, particularly the length of the organ containing erectile tissue (clitoris/penis) and how much of its length is visible. Of course, there's a whole range of externally invisible factors involved in sex development, including hormones, internal sex organs, and gametes (eggs and sperm). But the doctor, nurse, or midwife notes only what they can see and then makes a pronouncement: "It's a girl/you have a daughter" or "It's a boy/you have a son."

This pronouncement can be thought of as an ending (gender as fact) or as a beginning (gender as process):

- We can think of "It's a girl!" as *ending* uncertainty about what the baby is: She *is* a girl; she *will be* a woman. From this perspective, "It's a girl!" just shares factual information about the baby's gender.
- But we can also think of the pronouncement as a *beginning*: of the tremendous effort required to teach the baby how to *become* a girl who will someday *become* a woman, and what that looks like in this time and place. From this perspective, "It's a girl!" doesn't just share information but actually does something: It *signs up* the baby as a fledgling member of a particular gender category with locally specified rules for how babies of that category must be dressed, addressed, and engaged with.

The question of whether or not gender and sex are the same thing also separates the fact and process ways of thinking. If we think of gender as a fact, then reading an "F" sex marker on someone's birth certificate is the same as knowing they're a girl or woman, and reading an "M" is the same as knowing they're a boy or man. But if we think of gender as a process, then someone's "F" is simply shorthand for a quick survey of their external genitalia at birth. That isn't the same thing as a person's identity. Even though most female-assigned babies come to identify as girls and most male-assigned babies come to identify as boys, identifying isn't just "what happens" naturally. It's a process.

 WHAT DOES "INTERSEX" MEAN?

Sometimes external genitalia alone don't provide a clear-cut answer to the boy-or-girl question at birth. In these instances, a baby *might* be intersex. According to the Intersex Society of North America (ISNA), the word *intersex* describes "a variety of conditions in which a person is born with a reproductive or sexual anatomy that doesn't seem to fit the typical definitions of female or male." In a review of research published in the *American Journal of Human Biology*, Melanie Blackless and their colleagues estimated that approximately 1.7 percent of the general population is intersex. Alice Dreger, a bioethicist and former president of ISNA, and April Herndon, a former director at ISNA, point out the sheer variety of conditions loosely brought together under this term: "The medical names for various intersex conditions may refer specifically to the genotype (genetic basis), or to the phenotype (body type), or to the etiology (causal pathway of the condition), or to some combination of these. So saying someone is 'intersex' does not tell you anything specific about a person's genes, anatomy, physiology, developmental history, or psychology." Not all intersex people are identified as intersex when they are born; some might develop indications at puberty. Furthermore, some people identify as intersex, while others describe themselves as having an "intersex condition" or a "disorder of sex development." Phrasing varies depending on a person's own relationship to the term *intersex*.

The phrase *ambiguous genitalia* is commonly used when referring to intersex people or conditions, but it's a misnomer and considered offensive, as is the older term *hermaphrodite*. *Ambiguous genitalia* is a misnomer because not all biological variations under the intersex umbrella involve genitalia, as previously stated.

Distressingly, there is a history in North American medicine of irreversible genital surgeries on intersex infants, which, according to research by Human Rights Watch, is still ongoing: "Operations aimed at 'normalizing' these differences include clitoral reduction surgeries—procedures that cut and remove sensitive, erectile tissue in order to reduce the size of the clitoris for cosmetic reasons. Such surgery carries the risk of pain, nerve damage, and scarring, and yields no medical benefit." In the US, most of the recent bills that ban gender-affirming medical care for minors explicitly exempt these genital surgeries on infants. Many trans people see this as hypocritical because bill proponents claim to worry that children and youth cannot fully consent to treatment that changes their bodies. If a child or teen can't consent, can a baby?

Sociologists of gender describe the process of teaching babies how to be the gender associated with their assigned sex as a process of socialization. The teaching process happens whether or not people know they are participating. For example, psychologist David Reby and colleagues found that adults attribute femininity (if told the infant is female) or masculinity (if told the infant is male) to a baby by listening to their cry, even though vocal pitch differences don't emerge until puberty. In addition, psychologists Melissa W. Clearfield and Naree M. Nelson studied infant-mother play sessions with gender-neutral toys and found that the mothers spoke to, spoke about, and played differently with male and female infants as young as six months old—an age when their infants lacked any gender differences. From findings like these, we can take away an unsettling implication: We are often unaware of what we're teaching other people about gender or how we're participating in gender socialization.

Some would say that, because adults aren't always aware that we treat boys and girls—or babies presumed to be on their way to boyhood or girlhood—differently, differences between boys and girls must be "natural" (closer to gender-as-fact). Others believe that, actually, adults *learned* "how to treat boys" versus "how to treat girls" (closer to gender-as-process).

This brings us to another big difference between the fact and process ways of thinking about gender: what about gender is *natural* (often used to mean innate or biological) versus what about gender is *social*. This is often called the nature-or-nurture debate. In many years of studying and talking about gender with all kinds of people, I've come to see the "debate" as more of a continuum. Few people live out at the poles, and most pitch a tent somewhere in between, whether they're transgender or not. Where one sits on the continuum depends on many things, like whether one studied a particular discipline (for example, sociology and neuroscience have different knowledge bases about gender), how one's own experiences with gender have played out, and how gender is understood in one's culture or faith.

THE BIG GENDER REVEAL

Be honest: When you find out that someone you know has had a baby, what's the first question you ask? Chances are, you, like many people, ask whether the baby is a girl or a boy. From a gender-as-process perspective, we don't yet know the brand-new baby's gender, but perhaps only their sex. In a *HuffPost* piece, writer and new mom Jen Willsea breaks this down even further, asking, "Is it really anyone's business what sex my child has been assigned? Since gender is not knowable at this stage of a child's life (eleven weeks!), people are really asking whether my child has a penis or vagina. That is completely inappropriate and weird!"

Whether you agree with Willsea or not, consider the popular phenomenon of the "gender reveal party" where, originally, a pink- or blue-dyed cake covered with neutral icing was sliced at a party to "reveal" whether the baby in question was a "boy" or a "girl" based on a prenatal ultrasound in which external genitalia is visible or not. I have an active imagination and always pictured tense and furtive phone calls between obstetricians and bakery staff: "Do you have the intel? I have to get this into the oven!"

The gender reveal trend today has expanded from cakes to smoke bombs to dye-injected watermelons being fed to rampaging alligators, leading in some cases to wildfires and even deaths. Jenna Karvunidis is credited with creating the first viral "gender reveal party" in 2008, and in 2020 told *The Guardian* that she now regrets what she started: "You don't want what's between your legs to guide your path in life. I want my kids to grow up in a world where gender doesn't matter."

The next time you hear about a new baby, pay attention to whether the baby's "gender" is volunteered, even if you don't ask. I'll share more about asking gender-friendly baby questions in Chapter 7.

TAKING "NURTURE" TOO FAR: CONVERSION THERAPY

There has been a lot of research into the nature-or-nurture question, and great harm has been done in the name of finding the answer. Dr. John Money conducted now-infamous research on David Reimer and his twin brother. David was born with a penis and assigned male, but his penis was badly damaged in a circumcision accident. His parents sought guidance from Money, who suggested raising David as a girl alongside his brother. In the book *As Nature Made Him*, author John Colapinto documents the extensive socialization efforts on the part of Money and the twins' parents to "nurture" David into becoming a girl. Money published on the case and became very well known, but David struggled with and eventually rejected this forced socialization, coming to identify as a man. He would eventually commit suicide.

While Money's efforts with David aimed to socialize an M-assigned child into identifying as a girl (i.e., the gender *not associated with* his birth-assigned sex), the practice of "conversion therapy" has been administered to many children—both those who are transgender and who are gender nonconforming in their behavior, interests, or clothing preferences—with the goal of socializing them as the gender *associated with* their birth-assigned sex. Conversion therapy is defined as any treatment led by a mental health or medical professional with the intent to deter someone (often a child) from being transgender or nonheterosexual. Like Money's research, conversion therapy for transgender or nonheterosexual children and youth—or children and youth *thought* to be transgender or nonheterosexual—is an example of "nurture" gone too far. Often, transgender adults, some of whom survived their own experiences with this "therapy," have led efforts to ban conversion therapy. Some jurisdictions in the United States have outlawed conversion therapy, but it remains legal in others. Following the lead of survivors and authorities, such as the Canadian Psychological Association, the Canadian Psychiatric Association, and the Canadian Paediatric Society, the Canadian government legislated a ban on conversion therapy in 2021.

Biology and Socialization Affect Each Other

By now you've probably inferred that I'm closer to the gender-as-process or "nurture" end of the spectrum. But this isn't because I think biology and bodies are irrelevant. Many transgender people's experiences have shown that how people relate to their bodies is itself an ongoing process, not just "the way things are." As a result, it's uncommon to find a transgender person on either extreme end of the nature-nurture belief continuum.

The meanings and practices associated with things like muscles, body hair, and particular body parts come from a complex interplay of socialization and biology. For example, if you happen to have a penis, it's lots of fun to put out a campfire by peeing on it, but that doesn't mean standing up to pee is biologically necessary. And yet when a baby is born with an intersex condition affecting their external genitalia, one rationale given to parents for irreversible genital surgeries has been that the baby wouldn't be able to pee standing up. Somehow this particular way of penis-peeing has become intertwined with having a gender of boy or man, with a range of consequences for those under the boy/man umbrella. Some transgender men who don't have penises that urinate stand up to pee using specialized funnels because this can be an important part of being recognized as a man in everyday life.

The relationship between biology and socialization isn't complicated only for people who are transgender or intersex. The fact is gender is different in different places and at different times. When I teach about how gender changes over time and in different places, I like to use the example of women's eyebrows. Today, the prevailing eyebrow trend for women is bold, thick, and dark. I sometimes wonder whether women's eyebrows will ever stop expanding! But of course they will, to the great relief of women my age who plucked their eyebrows into oblivion in the 1990s so they could draw a razor-thin line instead.

Likewise, my own history with the hair on my face is a story of how our relationships with body and biology can be thought of as complex processes. In the middle of female puberty I was diagnosed with polycystic ovary syndrome (PCOS). My fledgling periods became unpredictable, and I began growing a beard. Today I love my beard and my modest moustache, and I keep both neatly groomed with barber scissors and lather shaves. But when my beard first appeared, it was abundantly clear that it was *not* to be loved.

First came the bleach. Next my mum took me to an aesthetician to have my beard waxed. Chin up, warm goo, then someone spanked me right in the face with a ping-pong paddle (that's what it felt like anyway). I was displeased. The aesthetician smiled brightly and reassured me that it was "for beauty!" Five more spanks and I was done, my face radiating like a hot plate while my mum drove us back home. This would happen bimonthly until I left home for university and found communities in which having a beard while not being a man was not only tolerated but also celebrated.

There is tremendous diversity among humans in how our bodies manifest things like hormones (both production and resistance), fertility, fat distribution, height, genital size and shape, vocal timbre, and hair. Absolute statements about "what women's bodies look like" and "what men's bodies look like" are easily disproved by looking around a crowded room. Yet this diversity most often loses to conventional wisdom, which recognizes only two rigid gender categories for all of these bodies. According to this "wisdom," bodies that deviate must be corrected—perhaps through clothing, beauty treatments, or even medical intervention.

However, some people—both transgender and cisgender (see the sidebar)—reject this "wisdom" and do not accept that their bodies need correcting. For example, since I was a child, I've tended toward things (clothing, activities, behaviors) considered to be masculine. This is one reason why I love my beard and why I also love the way PCOS affects my body shape—I tend toward having a belly and away from having hips. My relationship to my own body and biology has

WHAT DOES *CISGENDER* MEAN?

The term *cisgender* came into use in the 1990s to describe people who are not transgender, but has only become common in recent years. The prefix *cis-* comes from chemistry and roughly means "on the same side of," whereas *trans-* means "on the other side of." Unlike trans people, cisgender people have not traveled to the "other side" of how we commonly understand gender, but remain where they were expected to be from birth.

It might seem funny that the term for the "norm" (cisgender) was invented after the term for the "exception" (transgender), but this has happened before. According to historian Jonathan Ned Katz, writing tongue in cheek, "In the twentieth century, creatures called heterosexuals emerged from the dark shadows of the nineteenth-century medical world to become common types acknowledged in the bright light of the modern day," a decade *after* the term *homosexual* had entered *Merriam-Webster's New International Dictionary*. Similarly, *cisgender* was only added to that dictionary in 2016, whereas the editors claim *transgender's* date of first known use as 1974.

Although *cisgender* is a neutral descriptive term and not a term people have to take on or identify with, it has nonetheless become politicized. In June 2023, Twitter's new owner Elon Musk declared *cisgender* a slur on the platform, seemingly in response to frustrated trans people lobbing the diminutive "cis" at users posting anti-trans content, which is no longer discouraged to the same extent as before Musk's takeover. In a gender-unfriendly world, any word can become a weapon, I am sorry to say, even *she/her*, *he/him*, *boy*, and *girl*. Opposition to the term *cisgender* typically comes from strict "gender is a fact" views.

greatly changed over time, depending on whether I had access to a context where my body wasn't "wrong" because it didn't fit within the woman box. That I might like my beard or come to like it in time, that it might have a particular meaning for me, or that it might open up new possibilities for living and belonging: These were impossibilities.

And yet here I am.

DEFINING POLYCYSTIC OVARY SYNDROME

PCOS is a syndrome, or a cluster of symptoms that often co-occur. The Mayo Clinic's website suggests that a PCOS diagnosis is appropriate if a person has at least two of the following: irregular periods; excess androgen hormone (signs include "excess facial and body hair," acne, and male-pattern baldness); and polycystic ovaries, or ovaries that are "bigger. Many follicles containing immature eggs may develop around the edge of the ovary. The ovaries might not work the way they should."

Let's look more closely at the use of *excess* in the Mayo Clinic's description of facial and body hair. What counts as "excess" hair for people in the F box varies widely across time and across cultures. As we've seen in the case of intersex, biomedical practices are implicated in the process of gender just like other aspects of socialization. I've met people of different gender identities who have PCOS, but, of course, the vast majority of people with PCOS identify as women.

How Gender Works in Everyday Life

Whether you lean toward gender as fact or gender as process, there's no doubt that gender plays a key role in society. This book focuses on the *social* life of gender: on what you can do with language and various practices to open up gender and welcome all of the people and possibilities around you. For this reason, I'll leave behind the factor-process debate and delve into how gender works from a process perspective in everyday life. This is where and how you can make a difference.

Gender Is Everywhere
You probably don't spend a lot of time pondering your gender on any given day, but your gender is front and center in your life nonetheless. Did you enter your workplace at the same time as

another person this morning? You might have participated in a gendered ritual of door opening and door holding in terms of who walks through first. Looking for a snack at the grocery store? You might have contemplated—or altogether avoided—a healthy nut mix marketed specifically to women. Need a new pair of glasses? The store employee would probably bring you frames that are meant for either one gender category or the other.

There isn't necessarily anything wrong with this picture as long as others are reading us correctly. That said, I offer these examples to point out how deeply ingrained gender is in our lives, even if we rarely consciously think about it. As we delve into creating a more gender-friendly world, I'll invite you to notice the countless ways you interact with gender—most of which you probably don't even register. When you begin to notice manifestations of gender around you, however, you are better able to step back and assess how you might be participating in gender in ways that don't work for everyone. I'll describe two kinds of participation: visual and verbal.

Gender Requires Our Visual Participation

A neat trick of gender is how it hides in plain sight. Gender is everywhere, all around us, all the time, but we usually notice it only when someone is "doing it wrong." I don't mean *wrong* in the sense of "bad," but in the sense of "unlike most other people in the same category." If we had no categories, or even if the boundaries between the big two (boy/man and girl/woman) weren't so rigid, it wouldn't make sense to say that someone was doing gender wrong. They would just be doing gender in their own way! But these boundaries do tend to be rigid. This isn't because "they just are," but because we participate in keeping the big two categories rigid, intact, and separate, whether we know it or not. We can come to recognize when we are participating, and we can make different choices when we do (which I'll get into in Part 3).

With my students, who are learning to be teachers, I assign an exercise to help them reflect on these moments when someone nearby does gender (or another category) "wrong." I don't ask them to sit in judgment of other people, but to try noticing what their gut tells them: to ride the subway and keep track of when they do a double take or see something they can't wait to tell another person about later. Noticing is the first step.

The next step is trying to see *why* something triggered their gut response: Who stood out, what did they do, and what was happening around them? Many trans people know of certain times and places where we're likely to stand out—these tend to be boring places, like airports. The subway at rush hour is another one: where bored people exist in a state of mild anxiety because it's not easy or in their interest to leave, and in a state of mild irritation because it's not the most pleasant place to be. Beware of the bored in search of a stimulus, because it'll be the "different" person who stands out. Very often, it'll be me.

The last step is reflecting on what their gut might tell them about their readiness to welcome whoever walks through their classroom door. Through this exercise, students begin noticing how pervasive and rigid various social categories are, and how they unconsciously participate in maintaining them even if they're open-minded. This is because we're always on background alert for people and actions that go against our expectations. In fact, we visually assign others to a gender category all the time, but almost always unconsciously: in the background.

Picture someone who would immediately stand out to you in the gender department: someone who would prompt a double take, or who you might tell a story about later on to a friend (or even right away in a text message). I wager that something about their body (e.g., shape, height, presence/absence of facial hair, and/or voice) goes against the rigid rules for the gender category they are signaling with their clothing, grooming, walk, and/or mannerisms. Based on the visual information we take in, we assume we can deduce whether a person is "really" the gender they are presenting. It's kind of like when the doctor, nurse, or midwife makes the boy/girl pronouncement on the basis of (external) genitalia alone. We use very limited information to make a far-reaching judgment. It's easy to assume that the person you pictured (who would stand out to you) is transgender, but this isn't necessarily the case.

In the first edition of this book, I predicted that cisgender people would also be negatively impacted by anti-transgender bathroom bills in the United States, which mandate that everyone use the bathroom matching the sex marker on their birth certificate (often in states where this marker can't be changed no matter what). Among many such stories, *The Advocate* reported in 2022 that a twenty-four-year-old cisgender woman in Las Vegas—Jay—was misidentified as transgender and received transphobic harassment in a Rampart Casino women's bathroom. Jay chalks this up to having recently shaved her head. Being a millennial, Jay filmed the whole thing and uploaded it to TikTok, where it went viral. Casino security intervened, apologized to Jay, and handed the perpetrator a one-day ban.

All this is to say that many cisgender people are gender nonconforming: They do not look or act like what is typically expected of women or men. This can be because they dress, speak, behave, or accessorize in unexpected ways for someone of their gender. Or it can be for other reasons. Many cisgender women are tall with broad shoulders and deep voices, and many cisgender men are small and slight and speak with high voices. I wonder how bathrooms are working out for them these days in US states and other jurisdictions worldwide where transgender people are targeted by birth-sex bathroom laws. Of course, transgender people are most acutely harmed by such laws' demand for increased vigilance. But when the big two gender categories become more rigid, they become more rigid for everyone. When there is so much diversity among the bodies crowded into the little M and F boxes, hypervigilance is no one's friend.

Critically, when we take note of people who are doing gender "wrong," our reaction doesn't stay private. We usually communicate that we've noticed with our body language and our look. And once we've noticed, it's hard not to look again. Each of us has a go-to strategy for getting a sneaky second look at someone who stands out. We might *try* to be subtle because we know this can make someone uncomfortable. Pro tip: Your subtlety doesn't work. I will catch you, no matter how subtle you think you are, because I've had a lot of practice, like others who consistently stand out for any reason. A wonderful gift you can give to someone like me is skipping the second look and stewing away in your curiosity privately, so we don't have to know that you noticed. This is one way to change how you participate visually in the process of gender, and it is the first gender-friendly practice I'll share in the book, with many more to come.

Gender Requires Our Verbal Participation

So far, I've focused on how we participate *visually* in gender: based on what we see, and through our own ways of looking and orienting our look and our bodies. But there are other ways we participate in gender, or in the process of keeping the big two categories rigid, intact, and separate. We also participate *verbally* in conversations, whether with strangers or with people we have known for years. Just like visual participation, verbal participation includes how we react when someone steps outside of our gendered expectations. When this happens, we take note. When we take note visually, this is usually where it stops: with the looking. But when we take note in a conversation, a different kind of gender work happens, but the effect is the same: telling someone, likely not for the first time, that they are doing something wrong. Over time these messages can add up to a range of outcomes that can deplete a person's well-being considerably.

To flesh out what I mean by how gender works, I'm going to tell a story of how nontransgender people's experiences *can* be a way into understanding how gender can harm transgender people too. It's a story close to my heart: how my sister and I became friends. I share it with her permission.

Overlapping Gender Journeys: Coming Out As Nonbinary and Experiencing Infertility

I am the youngest of three, by several years. My older siblings are both straight, and neither is transgender. My sister, Megan, has always wanted children. In her late thirties, after a successful career in non-profit communications, she and her husband began trying to get pregnant. It didn't happen. In 2010 they began walking down the long road of reproductive assistance. First came intrauterine insemination (IUI), where conception happens inside of the body but with help. This didn't work, and so they began months and cycles of in vitro fertilization (IVF), where conception happens outside of the body and zygotes (sperm-egg combinations) are implanted in the uterus afterward. Eventually IVF was successful, and Megan delivered her twins in 2014.

I thought I had a good handle on reproductive assistance from seeing friends go through it, but I learned a lot from listening to my sister as she went through this experience on the way to having her twins.

In 2010 when Megan started down the road to IUI and then IVF, it was still an uncommon situation for people like her and her husband: straight, nontransgender men and women who make sperm and eggs in-house. Because it wasn't normal, it wasn't openly discussed. If it did come up, it was uncomfortable.

Standing Out and Getting Called Into Question

We know a thing isn't "normal" for people in a gender category if it stands out. For a woman in her late thirties, not having had babies yet made Megan stand out. People began calling her into question in everyday conversations: participating verbally in the process of gender by letting Megan know she was outside of the woman box. Near-strangers at the dentist or the hair salon would ask questions like "Why don't you have kids yet?" and "Aren't you having kids?"

Gender works in part through these verbal exchanges where someone's adherence with the rules or norms for people of their gender identity is called into question. It works even and often when the questioner has no idea that they're participating verbally in the process of gender: telling someone that they're doing gender wrong according to the expectations for people of that gender, in this time and place. It doesn't always take the form of an explicit question: "Why don't you have kids?" Or, even more baldly, "What's wrong with you?" Explicit questioning is one way of calling someone into question, but it can actually take many forms:

- **It can look like skepticism:** when you talk about something that's happening in your life and someone reacts like they don't believe it's happening to *you*, or like they don't understand why you would feel the way you do about it (happy, sad, indifferent, etc.).

- **It can also look like an exaggerated emotional response:** when someone reacts to your statement like you're talking about a tragic death. This lets you know that whatever you said—however ordinary to you—is the worst thing they have ever heard, which in turn lets you know that your own relationship to the thing is not normal. Usually this happens because a person is trying to display concern, but intention is only one component of how things go in our interactions.

- **It can also look like sharing advice or a story:** you tell someone about your persistent infertility, and they tell you about their past issues that were resolved by (insert strategy) and that you should try it. Again, this could be intended as a gesture of care, but it's also an effort to make *your* infertility either part of a more "normal" baby story (where women and men love each other, have sex, and boom) or a story that matches their own—a situation that presumably is more comfortable for the advice giver.

- **It can also look like silence:** when you talk about what you're going through to someone and make yourself vulnerable, but they say little in return, quietly nod and smile, or change the subject altogether. This lets you know that your life and what it contains are "too much" for normal conversation, even if you really need to talk about it.

An insidious part of standing out is beginning to isolate yourself. Once you know that you're likely to be called into question, you stop opening up to people about what you're going through. Many IVF journeys include devastating setbacks and experiences of loss. If you open up to someone, they might share a story about their one early miscarriage. Their story might be framed, kindly and unintentionally but still intolerably, as a lesson on how you should feel. Or they might just ask how you're doing, and probe when you don't talk about your infertility, because that's what "How are you?" actually meant. And then you have to tell them something. Or they might invite you to a baby shower.

Finding Spaces Where You Don't Stand Out

Consistently being called into question can lead to isolation, but it can also lead to startling connections with people who do *not* call you into question. Megan has never been embarrassed about infertility or accessing IVF and is committed to ending the stigma, which I greatly admire. She speaks freely about it to this day when she is called into question for having twins, another situation that reveals all sorts of invisible expectations. When Megan talks about how her twins are the result of IVF, her disclosure ruptures public-private barriers between strangers. People she has never met before respond by unburdening themselves with their own infertility stories. One time in a big-box store, Megan found herself in a tearful hug with a sales representative who told Megan about her own experiences with infertility.

Once her twins were born, Megan developed a tight-knit friend group of other twin mums. These ties have persisted over time. I've never wondered why Megan and her twin mum friends are so bonded. This is because I'm transgender. I, too, need spaces where the things I experience are normal. I need people I can talk to about these experiences without first saying what they mean. We all need spaces and relationships where we are not called into question, whether in small or large ways, because in some way each one of us is not quite the person others had in mind.

Finding Common Ground

When Megan began accessing treatment for her infertility, she and I were at the height of a drawn-out conflict that had festered since we were children. We were barely speaking, and when we had to, it was stilted or combative. Our battle had always been about taking up space and airtime in our family. We're both showboats, but my sister also works hard in the background of our family, whereas I, admittedly, do not. Megan devotes a lot of time and thought to how we're all doing, and I don't. Back in the day, I would show up, showboat, and fill the space, obscuring Megan's contributions. Of course, I didn't always see it that way, and Megan says she didn't see how she would become territorial.

Family therapy was instrumental in beginning to identify and work through this bad dynamic, but it didn't make us friends. That process started once we began talking to each other again, which happened to be while she was going through the worst of her infertility challenges and I was coming out as transgender, which at the time involved changing my name and pronouns. I did not anticipate that infertility and having twins would help my sister—a straight, nontransgender woman—understand what it's like to be me in the world. But it did. She began to connect the ways in which we are both called into question, every day, even if the content of the questioning is different. She came to understand how exhausting it was when people called me into question, visually and verbally. She began to see that this was exhausting even, and perhaps even more so, when the questioners didn't mean me any harm. And she began to anticipate and even get out ahead of some things that could have been harmful or just plain exhausting for me in the spaces we share.

By the time Megan's delivery date was scheduled, we were in a very different place in our relationship. I went out to Vancouver and spent time with her during the difficult, wondrous weeks after she gave birth and had two tiny babies to learn about and take care of. Ten years later, I can't remember that time without tears in my eyes. It remains one of my most precious experiences. Over time Megan has been instrumental in helping my other family members to use my name and *they/them* pronouns. Because of this experience, and from speaking with many others over the years about getting our name and pronoun needs met, I recommend that transgender people try tending to the relationships we have with people around us who we need to call on to meet our needs, and consider the particular history and dynamic of each one. There is always more to the story. I revisit this theme in the coda.

I shared this story in the first edition because I wanted to reach out to my cisgender readers who get called into question on the regular, and ask you to think about ways you might stand out from the norm, how others have called you into question, and how this question-calling feels. This seems to have worked. When I travel around in person (or virtually) to talk about the book, many cisgender women tell me how identifying with Megan's story was a turning point in their capacity to support the transgender people in their lives. I understand, as the reverse is true for me. More and more of my friends are having children in their late thirties and early forties. I can feel my way into these friends' experiences, holding space for somebody I love when they are experiencing IVF setbacks or when they miscarried a long-awaited pregnancy. I can do this without inadvertently telling my friend how they should feel (more on this in Part 2) or like they need to explain themself. I can do this because I am a nonbinary transgender person. I am an expert on being called into question, gender-wise, usually for worse, but sometimes for better when it allows me to connect in this deep way with the people I care about, including but not limited to the cisgender women in my life.

Each of us has a collection of awkward conversations and drive-by hurts from even well-meaning people. I ask you to rummage around in your own collection, and think about how a rigid, gender-*un*friendly world harms everyone, yourself included.

2.

Everyone Is a Gender Expert, Whether You Know It or Not

A Story: I Really Need Those Shoes

Drawing Your Gender-Friendly Road Map

Gender-Friendliness Is a Process

Gender-Friendliness: How Everyone Benefits

When I listen to trans people's stories of everyday life, I am blown away by the depth and complexity of our gender expertise: by what we know and know how to do regarding gender. We know how, when, and where to walk, speak, and act (or not) in order to just get on with our business like anybody else. We flawlessly intuit situations, we are fluent in nonverbal cues, and we anticipate most problems that come our way (or else many more of us would not be alive and thriving). There are infinite, undocumented ways in which trans people mentor and pass on these skills to each other. There are also many trans people who must learn for themselves. Regardless of how we come by this expertise and what we do for a living, all trans people, from fast food workers to stay-at-home parents to electricians to accountants to sex workers to secretaries to university professors like me, are gender researchers just because they live in a highly gendered culture.

You have this expertise, too, whether you realize it or not. In my experience, some people fear speaking up for transgender people because our issues seem so very mysterious and otherworldly: as though transgender people are on another gender planet, making a person feel like their lifetime of accumulated gender knowledge is irrelevant to what trans people experience. This might be due to a history of transgender erasure, including the actual erasure of transgender people through violence. But in my view, we (transgender people and advocates) aren't helping either if we ignore or belittle what *non*-transgender people know about gender's harms and constrictions.

In this chapter I offer some tools for *you* to begin naming your own knowledge and even expertise about how gender works around you. This expertise is a powerful tool in your gender-friendly kit. Parts 2 and 3 will offer additional and more practical tools. I begin with a story from my own childhood, and then invite you to apply its implications to stories of your own.

A Story: I Really Need Those Shoes

At nine years old I was about the same height as all of the boys I played with. I wore boy clothes and sneakers and had a short haircut. There wasn't much to set me apart, except for my name (a girl one) and being fat, a term I use without shame. I'm really good at sports as well as chubby. In fact, I was (and still am) proof that fat people can play and play well. But it's easy to take a fat kid down a peg on the sports field by reminding them that they're fat. You could take me down another peg by also reminding me that I wasn't a boy. All of this is gender-as-process playing out through question-calling, as I described. When you're a kid who is *always* called into question but can't change your surroundings, you look around for other ways to make it stop, which means trying not to stand out.

I started by trying to make the popular boys into my friends. I finagled after-school playdates with some of the king boys. But those playdates were awkward, and they didn't stop me from being called into question. If the boys and girls ever played together at my school, it was usually "boys chase girls" (or vice versa), in which no side was available to me. So I invented a complex role for myself:

both broker (helping chasers find and capture the chased) and spy (letting the chased know the chasers were coming).

I needed another strategy. That year the king boys were wearing Dr. Martens leather lace-up dress shoes. These shoes were not just ordinary boy-wear but a talisman of those on top. Only the ones who mattered had them: the ones who were team captains at recess, the biggest fish to catch when the girls gave chase, and those for whom boys and girls alike would show off. If I had Dr. Martens, I thought, enough of their magic would rub off on me and make me invisible: boy enough to not be called into question anymore.

I asked my mum. She said no because my feet were wildly growing and their $100 cost was ludicrous (in retrospect, I whole-heartedly agree). But my mum is lovely and kind and suggested a compromise: Let's go to Zellers (Canada's now-defunct Target) and see what they have. Predictably, Zellers was a bargain store and didn't carry Dr. Martens, but they *did* carry an off-brand alternative: Griffins. They were a bit narrower and shinier (due to the fake leather), and they lacked the trademark orange stitching around the sole. But this could still work, I thought optimistically. This feeling evaporated when the only ones in my size had soles that glowed in the dark. They were a sickly pus color in the daylight, and a nuclear neon green in the darkness of the janitor's closet. That's where I tried to entice the boys who instantly spotted my "glow-in-the-dark Docs" during their recess debut the next day. "Just come into the closet with me," I implored. Not remotely a cool girl, I came off like I was trying to play Seven Minutes in Heaven with the cool boys. An unqualified disaster. I stood out even more than I had before.

No matter my failure, this is *my* story of being a kid and knowing deep down that this one thing could make my life better at school in a way that directly related to the process of gender. Of course, a nine-year-old insisting that they *need* $100 shoes sounds like a spoiled brat to many ears. But underneath my insistence was a kid calling on their learned gender expertise to navigate my particular world of gender and make things easier.

What Was the Thing That *You* Knew Would Make a Difference?

It's interesting to look at gender from a child's perspective. Children navigate many different gendered spaces in an ordinary day as they move to, from, around, and out of school. They know how to make themselves invisible, safe, or even popular in each of these spaces—essentially, they learn how to do gender like other people there are doing it. Kids also know what would make them visible and incur the kind of unwanted attention that accrues to kids who stand out. Seeing other children be punished with unwanted attention because they stand out is a powerful hidden curriculum of schooling: something we're taught without being formally, explicitly taught.

We use different words for this unwanted attention when it falls on children and youth, as opposed to when it falls on adults. Among kids, we call this bullying. But in the workplace, when adults denigrate and isolate others due to their personal characteristics, we call this discrimination and sometimes, when warranted, harassment. This distinction is a topic of ongoing debate in many fields of study, including where I sit in education. Regardless of the name, these are varieties of question-calling.

My story was about shoes, but you probably also have a story about a thing that affected your ability to follow the rules of your gender category at school, in your neighborhood, or in another place where you spent time as a kid. As a child you had your own rich and remarkable gender expertise, which you acted on in one way or another. You retain this gender expertise today and have been deepening it throughout the course of your life.

Drawing Your Gender-Friendly Road Map

Part of your gender expertise involves recognizing and understanding how gender works around you—particularly how rigid and separate the big two gender categories are or how bad things get when someone steps outside of them. This is your starting place when you're setting out to make your world more gender friendly. In this section I'll lead you through a process of intentional reflection to help you find your starting place. You'll be drawing on your own gender expertise to draw a "road map" for your gender-friendly efforts. Then, over the course of this book, you'll learn strategies and skills that can help you implement action steps to follow your road map. We'll talk about those action steps in Chapter 8. By the end of this exercise you should have a sense of what could help and what could hinder your gender-friendly efforts, as well as some ways to boost the helpful factors and work through the hindrances.

The questions at the heart of this exercise are:

- How gender friendly is your space?
- How open is it to the many different ways that people live gender?
- Could this space welcome a gender-nonconforming or out transgender person, and could that person stick around and be okay?

Where Are You Now?

Think about one context where you regularly spend time. It could be your nuclear family, your extended family, a friend group, your workplace, a community organization, or a recreational space. In this space that you know quite well, let your mind wander through the questions in the following table, focusing on one person you know there in the M/boy/man box. Then begin again at the top and focus on someone you know there in the F/girl/woman box. The right-hand column offers prompts to get you thinking.

What gender expression changes would make this person stand out?	Clothing, hair, makeup, walk, voice, mannerisms
What new interests would make this person stand out?	Hobbies, activities, preferences, likes, dislikes
How long after the change would others call this person into question?	Immediately, after a few days, once X became consistent
What would that question-calling look and sound like?	Explicit questions, explicit concern, friendly reminders, new rules, laughter, gossip, pointing, sarcasm, eye-rolling, jokes, imitations, exclusion (active or passive), name-calling, theft or vandalism, harassment, violence
How might different people do the question-calling differently?	People in authority (boss, parent, teacher), people who are close to this person, strangers, peers
What relationships would change for this person?	Friendships, group memberships, intimate relationships, working relationships, roles, or responsibilities
Is there anyone here who could "get away with" standing out? Why?	
Who, if anyone, could make the question-calling stop? Why?	

The questions and prompts in the table are synthesized from a body of research on how people of all ages participate in keeping the big two gender categories rigid, intact, and separate. Even preschool kids have been found to do this kind of work: to call others into question when they step over a line drawn around their (perceived) gender category. Researchers in the social sciences use questions and prompts like these to study how gender plays out in a given setting, whether in interviews or when observing and taking field notes.

What Did You Notice?

You should now have a sense of what lines are drawn around M/boy/man and F/girl/woman where *you* are. You also have a sense of the consequences for standing out, including how different people might react. This means you have a sense of what the *expectations* are for people in the M or F box where you are, and can imagine what might happen to somebody new who didn't follow these expectations. Could that person stick around and be okay? Why or why not? Asking these types of questions will help you find the best routes and the biggest obstacles to gender-friendliness in that space.

The reflection exercise was all about someone you know making gender-related changes and beginning to stand out. But there's likely somebody in that space who already stands out. This person might be under the transgender umbrella, but probably not, because there are more cisgender than transgender people in most workplaces. In addition to helping you think ahead and hypothetically, the table can also help you think about who currently stands out where you are. Whose gender expression or interests are already called into question by others? What does that question-calling look and sound like?

One important note: Doing this exercise might feel like you aren't giving the people around you a chance, or that you're judging or assuming bad things about them and what they would do. If you feel this way, remember that you aren't dividing up those around you into good or bad people. You're just making explicit what you've always known about how gender plays out all around you. We all—myself included—participate in gender, and remembering this can help you have compassion for others who aren't yet on board. First and foremost, gender-friendliness is a practice of humility.

Who Can Help?

Let's now focus on the last two questions in the table: whether anyone could "get away with" standing out, and whether there is anyone there who could make the question-calling stop. I wouldn't be at all surprised if you answered both questions with the same name. In every space or community there are people who are only infrequently called into question, if ever. In my elementary school story, they were the king boys who wore Dr. Martens shoes and dictated the playground rules. If you focused on your family, they're likely to be an older sibling or a parent. In a workplace or friend group these people can vary.

What likely binds all of these people together—the ones who could "get away with" crossing gender lines themselves or who could make the bad things stop for others—is that they symbolize whatever is expected of people in their gender category in that time and place. I'll give you an example. Many schools in North America observe Pink Shirt Day, which is an annual event that commemorates an act of bravery by two teenage boys in Nova Scotia who wore pink to school after another boy—a new student—experienced gender-based harassment for wearing a pink shirt. Now imagine that some teenagers tried to have their school observe Pink Shirt Day, but the king boys (or men, like the gym teachers or football coaches) didn't participate. How long do you think the other boys would wear their pink shirts before taking them off? Conversely, imagine that the people organizing Pink Shirt Day *were* the king boys and men. Which observance would be successful, and which wouldn't? In answering this question you are using your gender expertise yet again and not just "common sense."

Maybe, just maybe, the person who could "get away with" crossing gender lines where you are is you. If it is, you've probably been struggling throughout the book to identify moments when you've been called into question by others. Or maybe it hasn't happened for a long time. Either way, you have a lot of power that you can bring to bear on making your spaces more gender friendly, and I'm very glad you're reading this book.

Gender-Friendliness Is a Process

My own stories of trying and usually failing to work the gender system of my elementary school are stark. This is because I stood out starkly, every day and in every way, as a girl-assigned person who didn't do girl in anything like the "right" way: like other girl-assigned people in that time and place. But we can't put people in two groups: people who stand out and are called into question versus people who blend in and are not called into question. Each of us hovers somewhere along a continuum, depending on how often we are called into question when we transgress others' expectations, and with what consequences. But we're all called into question sometimes.

Maybe you were the king or queen at school, whether for a little while or a long while: the person at the top, beyond reproach, who didn't have to call others into question to stay safe, higher than the "bully" who did have to do this because they weren't as safe or as popular as you. You were every bit as much of a gender expert as I was. The only difference is that you might have to dig a little deeper to identify what you did or what you were that put you squarely, resolutely inside the social safety box. Or maybe you don't. Maybe your girlness or boyness was called into question at home or at dance class or at baseball practice or everywhere else apart from school. Only you know, but you do know.

When we think about gender as an ongoing process of learning to do it "right," and of being taught or socialized by others when we mess it up, we begin to see this process at work in our lives. We're then less likely to explain away as natural consequences of innate sexed behavior the ways people hurt others, whether these people are us or those we love and identify with. This can be hard because it means recognizing that we *can* change, instead of thinking that we can't or even shouldn't change because this would challenge basic facts about who we are: Boys will be boys, and girls will be girls. It's doubly hard because we most often participate in keeping the big two gender categories rigid, intact, and separate without knowing that we are.

To be clear, this isn't about blame or shame. Our participation isn't our fault. Saying "our" is a deliberate choice to put myself alongside my reader and not above you. I have also participated in gender in ways that made it hard for others to live gender in their own way, whether this meant propping up the big two in mainstream contexts or maintaining the rigid, intact, and separate gender categories that have emerged in the 2SLGBTQIA+ (see the following sidebar) contexts I spend time in.

Like gender itself is a process, fostering a more gender-friendly world is also a process. It's easier to help make a more open and

 THAT ACRONYM, THOUGH

The letters in the 2SLGBTQIA+ acronym roughly stand in for *Two-Spirit* (see the sidebar in Chapter 3), *lesbian, gay, bisexual, transgender, transsexual, queer, questioning, intersex, asexual,* and *agender.* The acronym's meanings and inclusions change across contexts, and there is debate about how the acronym should be presented and whether it should be truncated (including with the plus sign, as I have done). To sidestep these debates, some use the phrase *gender and sexual minorities* (or a variation) instead. I tend to use the phrase *gender and sexual diversity,* which allows me to study phenomena (such as gender-based harassment) without relying on identity categories that might restrict my study to particular people or groups. When I do use the acronym, I follow others in using the plus sign for expediency.

welcoming world for people of all genders if you learn to tell your own gender story, and name and claim your own gender expertise. This begins with noticing how gender has affected your choices, your dreams, your relationships, and your desires: the ones you acted on and the ones you put aside. Whether you have generally benefited or suffered from gender and how it works, this book is for you. Not only will claiming your own gender expertise help make the world a more gender-friendly place, but it can also affect your own life in positive ways.

Gender-Friendliness: How Everyone Benefits

While this book is necessary in part because transgender-spectrum people are increasingly out and about in North American public life, there is a reason why the word *transgender* isn't in the title. This is because gender-friendliness isn't helpful only for trans people like (and unlike) me. There are compelling reasons to change our gendered language and practices even if there are no transgender people around for miles (which we can never know for sure anyway). This is because gender-friendliness can be good for everyone. How? Let me explain.

You'll Become More Forgiving of Yourself

Learning to recognize and change how you participate in keeping gender categories rigid, intact, and separate can help you become more forgiving of yourself. In describing visual and verbal participation in gender, I've focused on how gender works through interactions between people. But we also do gender to ourselves without any help from others. Each of us carries around a legion of people in our head and in our gut. They promote gendered standards for how we should look: for our body size and shape, and for our clothes, accessories, and hair. We discipline ourselves according to these standards and still more for our behaviors, desires, and even our feelings or responses to everyday and traumatic life events.

We're very good at calling *ourselves* into question, at letting ourselves know if how we look, act, want, and feel is not "normal," and with no help from anyone else. It takes a lot of time and energy to live up to the many rigid standards for people of your gender category, however that locally plays out (because it's different over time and in different places). I'm not suggesting that this is wrong or that doing gender by the rules can't be fun; it can be a festival of delights. And when it isn't, if you've developed a practice of trying your best not to call others into question, I wager you can come to notice when you're doing this to yourself and ease off a little.

You'll Enjoy New and Deeper Relationships

Another reason you might benefit from practicing gender-friendliness is that it could open up possibilities for relationships that just haven't shown up in your life yet. It can mean new and deeper connections with people you know, and new ones with people you don't yet know. There are many complex reasons why we drift into the lives we do, and why we linger and remain there or move on. Using gender-friendly language and practices is like running a different color up your flagpole. It's a signal of openness and an invitation to others who are generally used to being called into question, whether this means transgender people like (or unlike) me or cisgender people often told—explicitly or not—that how they look, act, want, or feel has to change.

If your way of being in the world every day doesn't serve up constant reminders—visually or verbally—that other people are doing it wrong, you might have a different experience of the people around you. When you do your best to stop being another medium for those messages, you may find yourself in new conversations and maybe with some new or deeper friendships. This is what started happening for me when I realized that the gender expertise I have developed as a trans person can help me to hold space for my cisgender woman friends who experience infertility. And because people called into question have to be more flexible and forgiving toward ourselves just to live life and get by, you might have help in bringing this compassion into your own relationship with gender. What a lovely (and gender-friendly) paradox.

Why This Book Doesn't Use "Ally" Language

One last thing before we move on to Chapter 3. You might have noticed that I don't use the term "ally" in the book, and this is a deliberate decision. There's nothing necessarily wrong with "ally" language. However, the term "ally" has a connotation of being apart or separate from a phenomenon that is causing harm to others. In this book, I'm centering how rigid gender rules and expectations affect everyone, including but not limited to transgender people. There is no "outside of" this phenomenon, even if some people are affected differently than others. *Gender: Your Guide, 2nd Edition* invites you to step into the work because you, too, have skin in the game, and not only on behalf of other people. Words like "coconspirator" or "teammate" are a better fit.

3.
Learning About the Transgender Spectrum

Why Are Some People Transgender? Because We Are.

Transgender People Are Diverse

Trans Kids in the Spotlight

Transgender People Have Many Ways of Transitioning

Media Representations of Transgender People Are Changing over Time

In this chapter I introduce the diverse spectrum of people who are transgender, meaning our gender identity does not align with the sex we were assigned at birth. I begin by defining transgender and introducing some of the diversity under the transgender umbrella. This diversity goes beyond most people's ideas about trans people taken from popular culture. I talk about processes through which different groups of trans people can come to understand themselves as transgender, including our many different relationships with the term *transgender* itself.

I then discuss transition. I try to strike a balance between providing information that can help you apply what you learn in this book and challenging the ongoing societal preoccupation with medical transition, which often diverts attention away from the barriers to full societal participation and well-being faced by many transgender people. Along the way I try to correct some common misconceptions and highlight trans people's different relationships with visibility and invisibility, which can change as we move among the different contexts of our lives.

Why Are Some People Transgender?
Because We Are.

You'll learn many things about transgender people in this chapter, but I don't address the *why* question: Why are some people trans and most people aren't? This isn't something I just left out; it's the result of a deliberate decision.

For over a century, researchers with different investments in the answer—including a desire to "prevent" or "reverse" transgenderness—have tried to find it. Many "answers" have been discredited. When I get this question, I follow the lead of scholar Susan Stryker, who coedited *The Transgender Studies Reader*, which consolidated the academic field of transgender studies: Focus on the fact that transgender people do and have continually existed, and work to ameliorate the barriers that we face. To quote Stryker's introduction to *The Transgender Studies Reader*, transgender studies scholars study "the many ways that relationships between bodily sex, subjective gender identity, social gender roles, sexual behaviors, and kinship status have been configured in different times and places," and document many attempts to snuff out configurations that didn't line up with mainstream views about gender. Sometimes the snuffing-out happened in people's own backyards, and sometimes it happened when European colonial powers enforced their own versions of gender on the people they colonized. I'm happy to say that, despite these efforts, many people we might now describe as somehow "transgender" continue to exist, as do many other ways of being a person who doesn't do gender in the usual way.

And so, when someone asks me *why* trans people exist, instead of answering this question I point out that we do exist and always have. In 2021, and for the first time, the Canadian household census asked and found that one in three hundred respondents is transgender. That's a lot of people, but still only those who answered honestly in front of the people they live with. Knowing that trans people exist, the more important question, to my mind, is: What can we do *because* that's true? I'm proud that my book sits alongside many other resources designed to answer this one.

Transgender People Are Diverse

In this section I'll introduce you to some ways that transgender people differ from each other in how we identify and express our genders. Transgender people can be men, women, both, or neither. I'll begin by describing the most common transgender pathways (F-to-M and M-to-F) and transgender people who are women or men.

I'll then move on to *nonbinary* trans people, meaning those whose path doesn't bring us (myself included) into the M tent or the F tent. I devote more space to nonbinary transgender people because we are still unfamiliar to many, both inside and outside of established trans communities. I share my own story of coming to be nonbinary because I'd like you to be able to put a face to the (nonbinary) name, particularly as many of the people who use gender-neutral pronouns, titles, and other things you'll learn about in subsequent chapters are, like me, nonbinary. In sharing my own story I particularly have in mind readers who may know none (or only one) of us at the moment.

Before I begin, I want to note that what I'll share with you here is limited in a few significant ways. First, it doesn't travel well. I'm writing from a particular urban, anglophone, Canadian (and North American) context, and I'm letting my own experiences shape the writing so that it's as accessible as it can be. But transness takes shape differently everywhere. What you've learned here might need some tweaks or renovations depending on where you go and who you meet. Second, the information I've shared with you isn't set in stone. This book is a guide to a particular moment in time, and some of these things have changed since the first edition came out in 2018. Change will continue, especially because the research on transgender

GENDER IDENTITY AND GENDER EXPRESSION

From here on out you'll be seeing the terms *gender identity* and *gender expression* a lot, and it's time to define them. Although these terms appear together in human rights laws across the United States and Canada, they have different origins and meanings and offer different kinds of protection. Because I'm a Canadian scholar, I'll share the Ontario Human Rights Commission's definitions of these terms, but these mirror definitions offered by American organizations, like the Human Rights Campaign.

"*Gender identity* is each person's internal and individual experience of gender. It is their sense of being a woman, a man, both, neither, or anywhere along the gender spectrum. A person's gender identity may be the same as or different from their birth-assigned sex." Gender identity protections are likely relevant only for people who are transgender.

"*Gender expression* is how a person publicly expresses or presents their gender. This can include behavior and outward appearance, such as dress, hair, makeup, body language, and voice. A person's chosen name and pronoun are also common ways of expressing gender." Gender expression protections are likely relevant for everyone, although their interpretation is in process at the time of writing.

Everyone has an *internal* gender identity, and for many of us this lines up with the gender category we were lumped into based on our assigned sex at birth. Our gender expression is *external*: how we communicate this identity to others.

people's lives and experiences is expanding all the time. And so, the best guide to what it means to be transgender is actually the experiences of the transgender people around you. In fact, how to learn and ask about gender where you are is something you'll get out of reading this book.

Transgender People Who Are Women or Men

Many, if not most, people under the trans umbrella were assigned the M sex and boy/man gender category at birth but are actually on the F/girl/woman side, or vice versa. Transgender people here tend to use identity terms that are familiar even if you don't yet know many (or any) trans people: terms like *transgender woman, trans woman, transgender man*, and *trans man*. Synonyms, sometimes used regardless of a person's age, include terms like *trans girl, trans boy*, and *trans guy*. In this section, I'm speaking across transgender women and transgender men in order to provide some foundational information, but there are significant differences among the experiences of these two groups. This is something to bear in mind and to expand on with further reading.

 WHAT ABOUT THE TERM *TRANSSEXUAL*?

Another term you've likely heard is *transsexual*, whether on its own, paired with *man* or *woman*, or paired with *M-to-F* or *F-to-M*. Foundational transgender studies scholar Viviane Namaste distinguishes between *transsexual* and *transgender* as follows: "The term *transsexual* refers to individuals who are born in one sex—male or female—but who identify as members of the 'opposite' sex. They take hormones and undergo surgical intervention, usually including the genitals, to live as members of their chosen sex. Transsexuals are both male-to-female and female-to-male. The term *transgender* is really popular in Anglo-American communities, and is used as an umbrella term to include all kinds of people who do not fit into normative relations between sex and gender." Namaste's definition of *transsexual* lines up with how many, but not all, people use *transgender man* or *transgender woman*. *Transsexual* is sometimes perceived to be an older term and less relevant to younger generations of transgender people. Regardless, it's important to be guided by how people use terms for themselves. If you're unsure what term is best, today it's safest to say *transgender*.

Coming to Know Oneself As a Transgender Man or Woman

Some research has been conducted with the goal of finding commonalities among the life courses of transgender men and transgender women. After surveying and interviewing thousands of transgender people in the early 2000s, researchers Genny Beemyn and Susan Rankin identified some milestones for different groups. The milestones for the F-to-M and M-to-F groups were similar but had some key differences. From a young age the people in both groups tended to:

- Feel and state a gender identity that differed from their assigned sex.
- Take some steps to repress or hide their identity.
- Go through a stage of learning and overcoming denial.
- Consider a medical transition (more on this later).
- Decide when and how to disclose their trans status.
- Come to "having a sense of wholeness" about their gender.

Even twenty years ago, there were emerging age differences among Beemyn and Rankin's participants. The older F-assigned transgender people tended to initially identify as lesbians, but this changed when they realized that F-to-M transition was possible. At forty, I know many older trans men who participated in queer women's communities as butches or masculine women because the possibility of being a transgender man wasn't widely known. Learning trans men are even a thing, at all, wasn't applicable to the younger trans man participants, who grew up with representations of transgender men as well as transgender women. I would venture that one of Beemyn and Rankin's milestones for M-assigned people or transgender women would also show age differences if their massive study was repeated today: "recognizing oneself as a transsexual rather than as a cross-dresser" (male-assigned person who sometimes expresses femininity but generally doesn't identify as a woman). The term *cross-dresser* is so far out of mainstream usage today, and awareness of transgender women and girls so widespread, that younger trans people likely do not experience this milestone at all.

That said, the different "sense of wholeness" milestones may resonate with "binary" trans folks today: "having a sense of wholeness as a different kind of man" (F-to-M) versus "having a sense of wholeness even when unable to be seen as a woman" (M-to-F) at all times, in all places. These descriptions reflect what the researchers learned about transgender men's and women's relationships with their bodies, and how transition doesn't necessarily enable seamless passing at all times for everyone because of the social meanings we attach to different bodies and body parts (as you saw in Chapter 1). That said, young people today increasingly see representations of, for example, transgender women in the public eye who flout expectations for "women's bodies," like Canadian multimedia artist and academic Vivek Shraya who regularly stuns on the red carpet and onstage in women's haute couture, proudly displaying her chest hair.

 ARE YOU ALLOWED TO SAY "QUEER"?

Yes. But let's talk about it some more. As an identity term, *queer* means, quite simply, "nonheterosexual," or not straight. Many older people (and some younger) have a negative association with *queer*, given its history as a slur used against gay people and people perceived to be gay. *Queer* is most often used as a slur in its noun form. Therefore, a good rule is not to use *queer* as a noun but to use it instead as an adjective, as in "the queer community." I tell my students that saying "the queer community" or "she's part of the queer community" is generally a safe bet because "the queer community" is a broad umbrella where a person might belong, not one specific identity that may be inaccurate. A person might see themself within the queer community, but they might personally identify with a different term. So, yes, you can say "queer," but *how* you say it matters quite a bit.

Visibility and "Outness"

There are important things to know about "outness" in relation to transgender people who are somewhere on the F-to-M or M-to-F side of things. Some transgender men and women seamlessly pass as cisgender men and women, respectively, and can choose whether and when to come out. Not all who pass are open about being transgender, and this can depend on the context: Sometimes they're out, and sometimes they aren't. Over half of respondents on the 2015 US Transgender Survey reported having to hide their gender identity at work, and a quarter hid that they had already transitioned. This can be called "being *stealth*," which is sometimes used to describe passing or not being out as a trans man or woman. Some people who are often or always stealth don't participate in the transgender community at all or do anything else that might "out" them as having a transgender history. Be careful with the term *stealth,* though, because many transgender people are uncomfortable with its implications of dishonesty. A person might identify as a woman with a transgender history (instead of a transgender woman) or a man of transgender experience (instead of a transgender man) to mark this difference: identifying as a woman who received an M sex marker at birth versus identifying *as* transgender.

Trans visibility has sometimes been politicized in community conversations. Some are committed to coming out and being visible as trans to push back against popular misconceptions that all transgender people want to pass, or that passing as cisgender is always the goal of transition. Interestingly, the adjective *transgendered* has fallen into disuse because it makes transgender sound like something that happened in someone's past, and not something a person is today. But *transgendered* might actually reflect some people's experiences, such as being a man with a transgender history rather than a transgender man. As with all groups of people, there's a lot that brings transgender people together and a lot that sets us apart. One thing that brings us together, I think, is rolling our eyes whenever someone insists that they've never met a trans person before.

Transgender People Who Are Nonbinary

By now you know that I'm writing this book from a double position: I both study gender diversity and I'm a transgender person. In this section I will speak about my own experiences because I'm nonbinary myself. Welcome to my house!

I situate nonbinary people under the transgender umbrella because we don't identify with the assigned sex and gender categories we were given at birth. However, I'll flag that there has been discussion among nonbinary people as to whether nonbinary falls under the transgender umbrella. Sometimes when I'm teaching, I draw a simple distinction—probably too simple—between "binary" trans people and nonbinary trans people. While "binary" trans people tend to be on "the other side" of gender (from that associated with their birth-assigned sex), nonbinary people tend to be on *neither* side of the binary. Some nonbinary people say that their gender is not "man" or "woman," and some say that they are not neatly or completely in either box.

I've put *binary* in scare quotes here because to my knowledge it isn't a term people identify with. (I have yet to meet a self-described "binary transgender person," which actually sounds a bit like a trans computer programmer.) "Binary" versus nonbinary is just a shorthand way to understand a key difference between these two trans families. You could say that the previous section was devoted to "binary" trans people while this section is all about *non*binary trans people. I didn't put *nonbinary* in scare quotes just now, though, because it is most definitely a gender identity that many people have.

In 2023, we know that the nonbinary population tends to be younger on average than the "binary" transgender population. In fact, at forty, I'm an elder in this community! I'm delighted about this because, as the baby in my birth family, I've always wanted to be older than I am. That said, don't walk away thinking nonbinary is just a newfangled thing the kids are doing. Nonbinary identities are more common among younger transgender people, yes, but this doesn't mean they're altogether new. I take great comfort in knowing that gender has always been lived in ways more diverse than powerful groups would acknowledge or just let be. Nonbinary may feel very new, but it's likely just the latest reemergence of something very, very old. References to people living gender in ways unrelated to "man" or "woman" are present in historical records and enduring unwritten knowledge bases all over the world.

Nonbinary Is an Umbrella

I'm using *nonbinary* itself as an umbrella term because people use different terms to articulate not belonging in either box. Every year since 2013 Cassian Lodge in the UK has run the Gender Census: an "annual survey of humans worldwide whose genders or lack thereof are not fully described by the gender binary." In 2023 the Gender Census was completed by over forty thousand people worldwide (in English). (Keep in mind that the survey is informal and not academic. That said, forty thousand is far higher than the numbers reached by many other surveys of trans people alone.)

Lodge asks respondents to select an identity word that best describes how they think of themselves. In 2023 Lodge offered eighteen words that have come into common usage in transgender communities and an open box for people to write in missing ones. The results align with what I've noticed in my community and in speaking with others across North America over the past decade. As you read the following results, bear in mind that people could choose more than one term. Over 60 percent reported that *nonbinary* best describes how they think of themself. Other terms chosen by at least a quarter of respondents were *GNC* (an acronym of "gender nonconforming"), *genderqueer*, *enby* (a shortened version of "nonbinary" preferred by some), *trans*, *transgender*, and *genderfluid*, which I address on its own in a later section. (You can see more of these results at www.gendercensus.com/results/2023-worldwide.)

Visibility and "Outness"

What does it mean to be out or "pass" as nonbinary? It can be hard to have people read and recognize one correctly as a nonbinary person. But let's think about what that even means for a second. Can we pin down "the way" that nonbinary people express gender? The answer is no because nonbinary people express gender in many ways. There are nonbinary people who express gender in a masculine way, and there are those who express gender in a feminine way. Some pass as cisgender men and women, to varying degrees, and have to come out as nonbinary in order for their gender identity to be known. Sometimes cisgender-passing nonbinary people have sought out transitioning strategies that contribute to their passing as (cisgender) men or women, and sometimes that's just how they look without any extra help.

When I think of how people infer that I'm nonbinary, when they do (which I'm happy to say is becoming more and more common), it's about more than how I express gender. My body gives off some rather counterintuitive signals, with or without clothes. For example, I have a beard, and it's very clearly shaped and taken care of. But this beard grows on a body that few people read as unambiguously "male." To make things even less clear (in the sex department), I always wear what is traditionally seen as men's clothing (e.g., I often wear a suit at work). Taken together, my body and my gender expression usually add up to people noticing themselves noticing: They don't quite know what's going on over here. I stand out, as I shared in Chapter 1.

Increasingly, people I meet are beginning to understand the way I stand out to mean that "he" or "she" isn't the answer. As awareness grows, the kind of thing that happened to me when a bunch of dudes were moving my partner and me into our new house can keep on happening: The gruff Jason Momoa look-alike charged with the heaviest loads gently pulled me aside out of the blue, apologized for having called me "she" before, and asked me for my pronouns.

To recap, there are many reasons why we can't necessarily "spot" nonbinary people, so being visible (or passing) as nonbinary is a bit of a misnomer. Some of us, like me, are being more commonly (and correctly) read as nonbinary. But for others who pass seamlessly as men or women, this isn't really happening. Of course, nonbinary people have different experiences of the world depending on whether we "look" nonbinary, which can have something to do with how our bodies and gender expressions play off of each other. I might stand out more, and that might make me more of a target in some ways, but it's also a little easier for people to infer and remember that I have gender-neutral pronouns. The reverse holds true for nonbinary people who look to all the world like garden-variety men or women. Some bad, some good, and for now, a lot of quiet time to recoup our energy in a world that still wants us to be one or the other, for gosh sakes.

Coming to Know Oneself As Nonbinary

Like Beemyn and Rankin's milestones for F-to-M and M-to-F people that I described before, their milestones for nonbinary transgender people (they used *genderqueer* as an umbrella term at the time) began with feeling and starting to express a gender identity other than the one associated with one's assigned sex. But that's where the clear similarities ended, particularly because the second milestone involved realizing that nonbinary is a "viable gender identity" at all. Alexander Tatum and colleagues analyzed data from the 2015 US Transgender Survey, comparing "binary" and nonbinary trans people's developmental milestones. They found the nonbinary people reported "feeling different" and thinking they were trans at a *later* age than the trans women and trans men respondents. Although kids today hear the term *nonbinary* growing up, that's very different from knowing that this gender is "viable" or real. For many outside of trans (and queer) communities, it is easier to understand how someone can be a transgender *man* or transgender *woman* than to understand how one can be nonbinary. For this and other reasons, many kids grow up without access to adults who know what *nonbinary* means.

Because there is a lot of diversity among nonbinary people, and because we're in my house, I'll share my own story—how I came to know myself as a nonbinary person. *Nonbinary* wasn't around for me to step into as a kid in the 1980s and 1990s, even if the phenomenon it represents has been around for a very long time, in different forms, all over the world. You already know a little bit about me as a kid, and that I chafed hard against the rules of the F sex and girl gender categories I had been assigned into. When I was in elementary school, my own participation in gender was devoted to passing as a boy, or at least boy enough to not stand out. Standing out in the gender department isn't fun for anyone, but at the time, the only way I knew of to not do girl was to do boy instead, as best as I could. My favorite auntie gave me an "all about me" poster when I was five or six. It had all kinds of speech bubbles, prompts, and questions for me to fill out. All I remember is the "three wishes" box and my top two: be a boy and have a dog. After much lobbying, I got the dog.

As I shared in Chapter 2, I didn't have a great time at my first elementary school. When I was eleven years old, my parents sent me to a late-start (i.e., not kindergarten) French immersion program across the city. My new class was very socioeconomically and ethnically diverse, and felt like a place for kids who hadn't fit in where they had been before. Although there were just four grade six and seven French immersion classes total in the program, it felt like being in an alternative school.

Many years later I'd work on a research study led by my long-time colleague and friend Liz Meyer, for which I interviewed teachers who have taught transgender and gender-nonconforming students. We found that alternative schools are places where these students are reportedly thriving. This was me. Gender wasn't as rigid at my new school, and so it was harder to stand out. I had a great time, and made connections that are important to me today.

When I think about my own gender history, I feel like grades six and seven at this school were kind of a sweet spot: I look back and recognize myself as myself. I wholeheartedly wish I could have stayed that person instead of having to re-find them later on. But as happens for many transgender people, the spaces of greater flexibility in elementary school didn't carry over into high school, which started in grade eight where I lived. For me, high school and puberty meant the onset of polycystic ovary syndrome, which I talked about in Chapter 1. And it just wasn't conceivable to my parents, doing their level best to raise a person they thought was a teenage girl, that my body shape and size or my facial hair could be things that helped me feel at home in my body and that I'd come to like about who I am.

And so, I started high school after a losing battle with Weight-Watchers, which I agreed to at the urging of my parents, believing weight loss would give me a "fresh start" at my new school. By a losing battle, I mean going from a big, butch kid with a big voice and a lot of confidence to an awkward wisp. Kryptonite. I actually stood out more and faced more question-calling as a wisp than I had as a big kid before. High school became more fun once I began the International Baccalaureate program in grade eleven, another alternative school within a mainstream school. Once again I met other nerdy kids from all over the city, and once again the rules for "cool" and "normal" were loosened to include different ways of doing boyness and girlness (still the only options). I got louder again. Being good at school, like I was, now carried prestige.

I'm lucky that I got to go to university, and that my family could afford to send me to university in another province so that I could freely move around as a young adult in a new place. I'd come out as gay before I left home, and when I got to McGill, I was quickly drafted into campus groups organized around gender and sexuality. In 2001 there was a lot of queer activism and there were many queer events on campus, but no visible transgender anyone or anything. By the time I left McGill after two degrees in 2009, this had changed. Transgender advocacy had begun to happen in student groups, and related positions and portfolios were being created within the university bureaucracy too.

While at McGill I had found a temporary home in queer communities as butch or masculine. When my masculine F-assigned peers began coming out as trans men during my generation's transgender "boom," I wondered whether that path was for me. We were learning that some of us had been boys all along. After all, I had that memory of being five years old and writing down my number-one wish to be a boy. I also cherished a memory from a trip to Los Angeles with my parents when I was seven. I took off my T-shirt at the beach and ran around all afternoon in my shorts and cycle cap, playing with a boy I had met that day and would never see again. Maybe because we were so far from home, no one made me put my shirt back on, and no one gave away my secret. Didn't all this evidence add up? I sure had all the signs that I was a boy too.

It was now very thinkable in my milieu to be a transgender man or transgender woman, but being transgender and nonbinary—in

 GENDER IDENTITY VERSUS SEXUAL ORIENTATION

I'm interrupting my story of coming to know myself as nonbinary in order to clarify something that you might already know: that gender identity (e.g., man, woman, nonbinary) is separate from sexual orientation (e.g., queer, gay, lesbian, bisexual). Imagine two piles of flashcards sitting in front of you on a tabletop. One pile has cards with gender identities, and the other pile has cards with sexual orientations. Any combination is possible, and all combinations exist. Just like there are cisgender people who are queer, for example, there are transgender people who are heterosexual: women who desire and partner with men, and vice versa. Transgender people have diverse sexual orientations just like cisgender people, and can be straight: not at all identify with or participate in queer communities. As you are learning, I am a nonbinary transgender person who also happens to be queer, but that's just me. Now back to the story!

neither gender nor sex box—was barely emerging. Social media wasn't yet a means of connecting with a world away from where you were, with the possible exception of *LiveJournal*, where many queer and trans youth created friendships and shared our lives with each other in sometimes excruciating detail. As a gender studies major, I read books by transgender people who didn't quite see themselves in the M or F box, like Leslie Feinberg. But they were famous. I was just some guy. And what I knew of trans life and what it could be in my context was "binary." I had the opportunities, knowledge, and community support to come out as a transgender man, but all I can say is that it never felt like the most urgent thing I had to do. And I guess I listened to that.

Nonbinary trickled into my consciousness. I didn't fully see or know that nonbinary was possible, was me, until a little after I had begun asking others to change the pronouns they used to refer to me. Even without knowing I was nonbinary, I knew that *she/her* felt odd and out of place, like I was wearing my T-shirt backward. I remember the first person I met who used neo-pronouns (*ze/hir*, in this case). I remember listening, rapt, to hir partner use hir pronouns in everyday speech. And I can indeed put my finger on the moment when singular *they/them* shone out to me like a beacon: when my then-girlfriend's younger sibling decided to try on *they/them* and see how this felt. When we first met, I'd immediately felt a deep affinity for this person, like we were peas in the very same pod. When the sibling began requesting and others began using their new singular *they/them* pronouns, I was flabbergasted. I couldn't believe how clearly I could suddenly see them. Singular *they/them* fit this person like a warm sweater on a cold day, and they seemed to me to be deeply, perfectly at ease. I couldn't unhear it, and no other pronouns made sense for them anymore. And so I took the plunge, too, and have never looked back.

When I was a new *they/them* person, there was nowhere I could send any of the people in my life who had practical questions about what my pronoun change meant: how to use my pronouns, how to talk about me, what other words they should use (because it was immediately obvious that gendered language is not only about pronouns). I often felt like an exhausted parrot after a long squawk. What I wanted was something that answered all these questions, which I knew weren't unique to me. But there wasn't a practical resource. There were only advocacy resources: on *why* meeting transgender people's needs is important but not *how*. That's why I founded *They Is My Pronoun* in 2012: the first Q+A blog on gender-neutral pronoun usage and user support. After reading around and engaging about gender-neutral pronouns with younger people on *Tumblr*, I learned about nonbinary. Just like my experience with having singular *they/them* pronouns, once I came out as nonbinary, I never looked back. Coming out as a nonbinary transgender person and hearing others use my pronouns, to the best of their ability, felt like looking at myself through clean glasses for the first time. I now know why I haven't pursued a binary transgender path that could take me firmly into the M box, and I know why I chafed in the F box for so many years. I know why my body felt right even when all the messages told me otherwise, from the ones I received from WeightWatchers and aestheticians to the ones I received when my trans guy friends began hormone therapy (more on this to come) and projected their excitement at their own masculinizing bodies onto my own, which stayed the same. I know why there are gendered rituals I want to be exempted from and others I want to keep participating in: why I have no wish to attend all-women things, and no wish for automatic inclusion in all-men things either. This gets me out of all kinds of situations that, frankly, a lot of people find boring (not just me). It also means I get to approach gender like a buffet (taking what I love and leaving the rest behind), and that I get to connect with men, women, and other nonbinary people in ways I never thought possible. It means I get to feel like a bit of a gender wizard who has been on so many sides of this thing and seen it from so many angles. And I know this helps me do my job, whether I'm teaching, advocating, or doing research on gender in education.

Keep in mind that this is my story, not a template for everyone. Some nonbinary people come to their gender identity in a meandering way, like I did, or later in life once they realize that this is possible, and some people meander a lot less. Increasingly this is because kids are growing up in a world where they can know about the possibility of living gender in their own way. Today kids can do what I and others could do only in our midtwenties: see how this feels and see if it fits.

A friend sent me an article from *Tablet*, an online magazine, about a Jewish transgender teenager named Enoch Riese, who is nonbinary and uses *ze/hir* pronouns (which we'll explore in Chapter 4). Enoch approached hir rabbi about how ze could participate in the Jewish coming-of-age ceremony that is usually divided along binary lines: bat mitzvah for girls and bar mitzvah for boys. Enoch's rabbi rose to the challenge and found a way forward that was appropriate for Enoch's nonbinary gender identity while also appropriately grounded in Jewish tradition. All over the place, in every aspect of our lives, nonbinary people are seeing others step up and respond to the challenge of making previously binary-gendered things open to us too. Enoch's story offers just one example of a gender-friendly practice, and I have many more examples to share with you.

I'm going to go ahead and push pause on my own story for the moment, but when we come to the topic of transition, I'll be back.

Transgender (and Other) People Who Are Gender-Fluid

So far in this chapter I've introduced you to two major pathways taken by people under the transgender umbrella: "binary" and, just now, nonbinary. Before I move into the next section on transition, though, I need to unsettle an assumption that might have been building: that transgender people's pathways are necessarily one-way tickets, or that all trans people do gender in the same way all the time once we've found a way that feels right.

First of all, as I pointed out in Chapter 1, gender isn't really a static thing for anyone, whether you're transgender or cisgender. When we think of gender as a process that we all participate in, we come to see that everyone does gender a little differently as we move among the spaces we spend time in, and also over our life course. This isn't just a trans-people thing. Both cisgender and transgender people fluctuate in our gender *expression*—in our clothing, grooming, behavior, and body language—but for most of us this fluctuation happens within a limited range. This includes me. My gender expression is on the masculine side, but flamboyantly so. I love bright colors and big prints. (To my partner's chagrin, I love pairing them even more.) While my masculine gender expression shows up differently depending on where I am and what I'm doing there (at work, at the gym, at a bar, giving a talk), it's still generally masculine and I'm still wearing men's clothing. This stability works for me and for most other people, too, whether transgender or cisgender.

A third transgender-spectrum pathway, then, is gender fluidity. People who are gender-fluid are people whose gender expression and/or gender identity don't park in any one place, or at least not for long. A gender-fluid person may have a gender identity, or internal sense of themself, that sits still (e.g., woman, man, nonbinary, etc.) while still moving all along the masculinity-femininity spectrum (including both/neither or androgyny, in the middle) in their gender expression. A person's gender-fluid expression can also collage many different ways of doing gender at any one time.

People can express gender fluidity regardless of whether they identify as a man or a woman, whether they are cisgender or transgender, and also whether they are "binary" or nonbinary. For example, a person assigned M at birth with a boy or man gender identity can be gender-fluid in his gender expression. An example in the public eye today is singer Harry Styles, who broke many boy teen idol rules by posing for a 2020 *Vogue* cover in a Gucci dress. Harry is also regularly photographed going about his day or out to the club in crochet tops and sparkly shorts, and on another day in typically masculine fashion. Whereas gender-fluid people like Harry Styles and others *express* gender in a fluid way, some people under the transgender umbrella *identify* in a fluid way. This means their gender identity—internal sense of themself as a man, woman, nonbinary, etc.—changes. People with gender-fluid identities may express gender in a variety of ways (just like everyone else).

Trans Kids in the Spotlight

So far, what I've shared about transgender people has spanned all age groups. Today, however, we know much more about transgender children and youth than ever before, including that trans kids are not by any means new, as historians have demonstrated. Scholar Jules Gill-Peterson did extensive research in US gender clinic archives and found evidence of transgender children living in their self-identified genders as early as the 1930s. This makes sense if you think about it. In the 1950s, many adult patients of these clinics reported knowing they were (what we now call) transgender when they were children.

This probably comes as a surprise: Trans kids are in the historical record! It's likely surprising because today's transgender kids are often positioned as a newfangled thing by polarizing and often partisan rhetoric. I know trans kids aren't new because I was one in the 1980s. I knew who I was and wasn't but lacked any language to describe how I felt, as did the adults around me, so I was funneled into a path that wasn't for me. I recently went through family photos to make the slideshow for my dad's celebration of life, and it was hard to see myself change from, well, *me* at ages five (post haircut) through twelve into someone I barely recognize for most of my teen years. I remember feeling lost, uncomfortable, and out of place in relation to my own body and other people around me. I had no access to trans people's rich lives and our long histories, and while my challenging experiences made me who I am, there are things I would gladly let go of if I could have been affirmed instead.

I get how trans kids can *seem* new if you don't have all the information. As early as 2018, researchers in Pittsburgh found that one in ten students in the city's public schools reported a gender-diverse identity (which can mean many different things, as you know), and this number was higher among youth who are not white. Many more transgender youths than adults before them come out as *neither* girls *nor* boys because they are among the first to grow up knowing that nonbinary (etc.) is a gender and a possible life. This includes the nonbinary teen at one of my workshops who, six years ago, told me *they didn't know they could be out and have a job until they met me.* Think about it. For all these reasons, I was unsurprised that, on the 2021 Canadian national census, two-thirds of the transgender or nonbinary respondents were under thirty-five.

Just because more trans kids know who they are today doesn't mean there weren't trans kids before. While many young trans people know who they are earlier in life, more and more parents are also willing to affirm their kids' gender identities. For years now, cisgender parents have watched trans people on TV, worked alongside us, and maybe even sat beside us at church or cheered on our kids, too, at the baseball game. What's more, laws now require school districts across Canada and in places across the US to protect students from discrimination because of their gender identity and gender expression. Being called the wrong name and pronouns, having to use the wrong bathroom, and being told that you can't wear a particular uniform—these are examples of possible discrimination, and many schools work to prevent and respond to them. This means that more and more trans kids are also being affirmed at school. If a kid is really lucky, they have overlapping support: affirmed both at home *and* at school.

We also know more these days about children's gender identity development, including from Dr. Kristina Olson's research with large samples of transgender and cisgender kids who her research team has been following for years. Dr. Olson's studies have shown that trans kids who live in their gender identity have developmentally normal rates of depression, but trans kids who don't socially transition (more on this topic later) have higher rates. Her research also suggests that transgender *and* cisgender kids' gender identities and gender-related preferences remain stable in childhood, speaking back to misinformation about transness being a "phase" or a "fad" in children. Despite living in scary times for trans kids and their families, particularly in the US, the gender-friendly best practice grounded in research and relevant professional expertise is following a child's lead and affirming the gender they tell us about as opposed to the one we (adults) expect them to have.

Transgender People Have Many Ways of Transitioning

I feel like transition has been a bit of a shadow topic so far, popping up here and there. It can sometimes feel like this is the only thing that cisgender people really want to know about, and that *transition* is just shorthand for information about extremely personal parts of our bodies. Why the fixation? What do we think we know about someone when we think we know about (let's be honest) their junk? After all, most of the time gender plays out in everyday life with everyone's clothes on. I don't need to see a vulva before saying *she/her* pronouns.

That said, a reason why many of you picked up this book is to understand what to do about gender diversity in everyday life. If we notice ourselves trying to infer another person's gender, that means they stand out. And so, it's important to understand some basic information about transition because it's relevant to why some transgender people stand out to you, stand out differently, or don't stand out at all. These differences can help us to know when it's time to rethink or be particularly mindful about our language and practices. In an era of increasing polarization and misinformation about transgender people and our transitions, particularly trans kids, accurate information about transition is also an essential part of your gender-friendly tool kit.

A common way to explain the process of transitioning is to draw a distinction between social transition and medical transition. Transgender people across the different groups under the "T" access different social and/or medical transition strategies, and each for our own reasons. The goal of transition is often articulated by transgender people as something like greater alignment among our gender identity, our body, and how other people see, interpret, and relate to us in everyday life.

Social Transition

In the updated second edition of *Trans Bodies, Trans Selves*, a comprehensive handbook for diverse transgender people on how to be and stay well, the sections on social transition and medical transition give a helpful sense of how many people in trans communities understand the distinction. Here are the social transition strategies discussed at length in that book:

- Names
- Pronouns and gendered labels
- Clothing
- Makeup
- Hair, including wigs
- Packers (gives the appearance of penis and testicles)
- Stand-to-pee devices (in order to use a urinal)
- Breast forms
- Binders (minimize the appearance of breasts)
- Tucks and gaffs (minimizing the appearance of penis and testicles)
- Hip and butt padding
- Bodily modifications like tattoos and piercings, which, for some, are gender-affirming

To this list, I would only add removing facial or body hair through electrolysis, or beginning to encourage our body's natural hair to grow (for example, if a female-assigned trans person stops plucking, shaving, or bleaching formerly "unwanted" hair). Social transition can be loosely mapped onto the concept of gender expression that you've seen throughout the book: how we use things like clothing, hair, facial hair, nails, makeup, etc. (whether their presence or absence) to communicate our gender identity to those around us so that they address and engage with us in ways that feel right. It's interesting to read this list and think about the padded push-up bras or curve-enhancing jeans frequently worn by cisgender women to express gender!

"Social Transition" chapter authors Florence Ashley and Avy A. Skolnik also list behaviors that can change as part of social transition. Demeanor, especially how we position our arms when relaxed, move our hands, or walk, is deeply gendered (not innately sexed), as are the pitch, intonation, and resonance of our voice, which can all be changed with training and practice. Learning to navigate others' expectations for the gender you are now being read as is also part of social transition, as is learning to play by these expectations—or at least know when you are being held to them, and with what consequences—in gendered spaces that are new (to you).

Things that transgender people take into consideration when planning for social transition include:

- **Supports:** This includes thinking about whether we have enough support where we are and whether we might experience discrimination.
- **Cost:** Social transition can cost a lot of money. Things like buying an entirely new gender-appropriate wardrobe and hair removal can be key to one's sense of wholeness and alignment, not to mention safety. When transgender people control access to transition-related resources, these things are often subsidized just like medical transition strategies (if not covered by government or private insurance). Colleges, unions, and other organizations sometimes offer these subsidies.

Medical Transition

Medical transition is just what it sounds like: strategies that necessarily involve medical professionals. Generally, only surgeries and hormones fall under the medical transition header.

When they hear "transition" in the context of transgender people and issues, most people think about one thing: The Surgery. This reveals three common misconceptions about transition:

1. Transition *necessarily* involves surgery in the first place.
2. Transition *necessarily* involves only one surgery (if surgery is sought out).
3. There is *a* surgery that *all* transgender men and transgender women seek out, respectively. (This misconception also excludes the possibility that nonbinary people would seek out gender-affirming surgeries. Some do, myself included.)

All are false. Transitioning *can* involve surgery for some trans people, but not always. Ian Nolan and colleagues reviewed all available research on this topic in 2019, including the landmark 2015 US Transgender Survey. They estimate that between 25–35 percent of transgender people in the US have accessed gender-affirming surgery, with only 4–13 percent having accessed any kind of genital surgery. However, these are older numbers; results from the 2022 US Transgender Survey were due out in 2023 and will shed even more light on trans people who pursue surgery as part of their medical transition, and those who don't.

Over time in transgender communities a surgery vocabulary has emerged that makes it clear what's being talked about without relying on terms that may not line up with people's gender identities. For example, a common conversation topic among many transgender people who were assigned female at birth is "top surgery," or the surgical removal of breast tissue. Among transgender people assigned male at birth, though, "top surgery" might mean breast augmentation. Trans people also often use the term *bottom surgery* as shorthand for many genital surgery options that have become available over the years. However, we no longer think of transgender surgeries as including just top and bottom surgeries, or only affecting people's primary or secondary sex characteristics. Transgender surgeries can also include cosmetic surgeries, like facial feminization surgery, liposuction, and surgeries to the hands.

With or without surgeries, medical transition may also involve hormones. This can mean hormone replacement therapy (HRT) or taking puberty-suppressing hormones (sometimes called hormone blockers). HRT involves taking a feminizing hormone (usually estrogen) or a masculinizing hormone (usually testosterone). Different transgender people, whether "binary" or nonbinary, take hormones for different reasons, for different lengths of time, and sometimes on and off. A person might begin taking estrogen or testosterone, reach a desired degree of feminization or masculinization, and then stop once an irreversible change like voice-deepening (on testosterone) has happened to a level they are comfortable with. Another example is some transgender men who wish to become pregnant or freeze their eggs going off of testosterone for a period of time. Some people take hormones all of their lives, and some do not. Whereas HRT is additive, taking hormone blockers is preventive. Blockers prevent someone's body from absorbing the masculinizing or feminizing hormones it was already producing. Blockers are sometimes prescribed to transgender adolescents for short-term use in order to delay all the complications puberty can bring when your body starts doing things that clash with who you know you are. The World Professional Association for Transgender Health's (WPATH) *Standards of Care* contain strict guidelines for doctors in prescribing hormone blockers to adolescents, even though they are fully reversible.

Because the purpose of this book is to help you think differently about how we presume, engage, and deal with gender in everyday life, and because everyday life very seldom requires knowing about things like people's access to surgeries and hormones, I'm going to leave further explanation of medical transition to existing resources like *Trans Bodies, Trans Selves*. I highly recommend it for further reading.

How to Talk About Transition

While common knowledge about transgender people is increasing, I've seen how even people who are at ease saying terms like *transgender* and *trans* can feel awkward or unsure of themselves when it comes to talking about transition. In the trans communities I'm part of, we usually use variations of the verb *to transition*, as in: "K is transitioning," "when K was transitioning," etc. This is useful because you don't have to reference K's assigned sex at birth, which is nobody's business. This strategy doesn't assume K is on a "binary" path either. Here are some things to avoid:

- Don't use phrases like "K is becoming a [gender]" because this may not reflect K's own understanding of their gender and transition, and speaking for someone else is never a good idea.
- Don't use *transgendering* as a verb.
- Honor that K's transition is their business, and do not share any specific information that you are privy to. Unless K has explicitly said that you may share information about their transition, whether social or medical, consider this private.
- I can't think of any reason why you might be talking about another person's surgeries, except if you are part of their care team during that process. That said, if you need to refer in a general sense to surgeries that are part of medical transition for some transgender people, a phrase used by many of us is *gender confirmation surgery* or *gender-confirming surgeries*. Avoid outdated terms like *sex change* and also avoid discussing *the surgery* in a singular sense, which you now know reflects many misconceptions.
- Lastly, transition is not a black-and-white, open-and-shut, or linear thing for many transgender people. There are as many ways to experience and plan for one's transition as there are ways of being a transgender person, whether one is a man, a woman, a nonbinary person, or none of the above. It's best not to ask someone about their transition unless they explicitly

volunteer information about it, and not to ask about the outcome or "when it'll be over," which is basically another way to tell someone who they are without meaning to (as I discuss in Chapter 7) because you're effectively telling them that they aren't there yet!

The Regulation of Gender and Transition

Many transgender people's experiences of and access to transition have been greatly affected by how the North American (and other) medical and psychiatric authorities have sought to regulate gender. For a long time, doctors and psychologists tightly controlled access to medical transition in particular, and the only acceptable goal of transition was passing seamlessly as a cisgender man or woman. For most of the twentieth century, and also to this day in some places, transgender people's access to strategies that allow many of us to find wholeness and happiness in our own bodies was dictated by other people: by these gatekeeping professionals. Often according to restrictive legal standards, gatekeepers would prescribe surgeries that were medically unnecessary and unrelated to a trans person's own identity and relationship with their body. In many places, for example, transgender men were made to undergo hysterectomies before they would be granted legally recognized documentation recommending a change to the sex marker on their identity documents. Today, however, many transgender men don't have hysterectomies, and some elect to give birth.

Similarly, many transgender women have been made to undergo complete orchiectomy and vaginoplasty before they could receive medical or psychiatric dispensation to change the sex marker on their documentation, regardless of their own desire to do so. Transgender people and supportive healthcare professionals have lobbied long and hard for these harmful rules to change, and the current best practices for transgender healthcare are now found, as mentioned previously, in the WPATH *Standards of Care* (www.wpath.org/publications/soc). The WPATH standards are developed by a team of professionals that includes transgender people, and do not require any transgender person to undergo irreversible medical interventions that don't match how they actually relate to their own body.

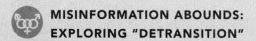

MISINFORMATION ABOUNDS: EXPLORING "DETRANSITION"

While the vast majority of trans people who pursue social and/or medical transition look back and see marked improvements in their well-being and mental health, some people decide to stop a transition. This can happen for many reasons, and a significant one is experiencing anti-trans discrimination or a lack of support from one's family or friends. A trans person might also cease hormone therapy that had been supporting a "binary" transition (i.e., were identifying as a trans man or trans woman) if they realize they are actually nonbinary.

These reasons aren't the same as "Whoops, I'm not actually trans" or altogether regretting transition. Of course, being mistaken and having regrets are part of every human experience. The National Center for Transgender Equality illustrates an essential irony: "One Dutch study of nearly seven thousand transgender people found that the rate of regret was less than 1 percent among those who received treatment as adults—and there were no cases of regret among those who received care before the age of eighteen....Up to 30 percent of knee replacement patients regret getting surgery—but no one's trying to ban those!"

Anti-trans campaigns aiming to ban gender-affirming healthcare for trans kids and adults in the US seize on detransition as a culture-war weapon. In this context, people whose gender journey includes detransitioning—for any reason—or retransitioning are often held up as anti-trans symbols, when their healthcare and social support needs are actually strikingly similar to other people of trans experience. People who detransition or retransition may also need access to gender-affirming medical and mental healthcare, so anti-trans campaigns that purport to respond to these people's needs are likely harming them in the process.

The Role of Medicine and Psychiatry in Defining Transgender

One reason why the medical and psychological gatekeeping regime existed was because transgender people had to meet the criteria for a psychological disorder before being granted access to transition. In 1980 "transsexualism" and "gender identity disorder of childhood" were added to the third edition of the American Psychiatric Association's *Diagnostic and Statistical Manual of Mental Disorders*. "Transsexualism" was eventually dropped in favor of "gender identity disorder," and in the fifth edition, published in 2013, the "disorder" language was replaced by the current term: *gender dysphoria*. This has been praised by some in transgender communities because for the first time being transgender itself is not branded a disorder unless one experiences gender dysphoria, or, loosely, a pervasive feeling of unhappiness with one's body and/or assigned sex or gender category. Not all transgender people experience dysphoria. For some who do, medical transition is a proven successful treatment for gender dysphoria, as is social transition.

One way in which transgender people resisted and successfully manipulated the gatekeeping regime was by learning to tell the kind of story that professionals wanted to hear. This story became a kind of genre that transgender people would teach each other to recite in order to access the transition strategies they desired, even if these came with things like unwanted surgeries that were less desired by an individual or not desired at all. The story usually contained motifs like "having always known since childhood" and "being trapped in the wrong body." While these motifs certainly do resonate with some transgender people, they do not reflect everyone's experiences. In fact, some people connect the recent and increasingly public (re-) emergence of nonbinary transgender people with the gradual demise of the gatekeeping regime in many contexts, and with the increasing self-determination and control that transgender people are able to exert over our own healthcare alongside supportive professionals. In Canadian provinces and territories, and in many

American jurisdictions, being recognized as transgender no longer requires one to access a diagnosis of any kind or pursue any kind of medical or psychiatric intervention unless warranted by one's particular circumstances.

To this day, however, transgender people's access to transition still varies considerably from person to person based on whether someone has healthcare coverage from a government or an insurer, and whether accessing hormones or surgeries would jeopardize things like personal safety, housing, employment, and crucial relationships. This will be made abundantly clear in the next section when I return to my own gender story.

Why Medical Transition? My Story Continues

By now I hope it makes sense when I say that "transgender" can mean different things to different people, and so can transition. For example, many female-assigned transgender people (including trans men and nonbinary people) have top surgery and take testosterone, but some do just one of these things or do neither. If you're a transgender man and you do both of these things, your body shape and facial hair can change and make it more likely that people will see and gender you correctly. Many transgender men also experience welcome changes in how they feel, not just how they look.

But passing as a (cisgender) man may not be the main reason someone takes testosterone or has top surgery. In particular, having breasts and keeping them comfy typically means supporting them somehow, and the garments used—whether we call them bras or binders—can be tremendously uncomfortable. Garments aside, just having breasts can be uncomfortable and even painful. For some female-assigned nonbinary transgender people, breasts can be—literally—a pain in the neck. This sounds trivializing, but it resonates with how I felt for a long time: that breasts were just a pain in the neck to be tolerated. It took me until 2020—two years *after* this book's first edition was published—to realize that I needed top surgery in order to be fully at home in my body as a nonbinary person.

I'm typically a slow and organic decision-maker who waits for things to feel right. By summer 2019 my relationship with my chest meant that I was making a semiconscious decision to never wear T-shirts outside of the house, only roomy button-downs that didn't reveal my chest contour. I had chronic neck and shoulder pain from fifteen years of first wearing binders and then the tightest, most restricting sports bras I could possibly find when binders became too painful. The most basic Nike sports bra worked best, but every few years they would tweak the model: add "chicken cutlets" for padding or pleated stitching that makes contained boobs more obviously "boob-shaped." No, thanks. I was a university professor wearing custom suits on the outside, but my disintegrating old Nike sports bras would shed bits of elastic all over the floor as I got ready for bed at night.

During the worst of the COVID-19 pandemic, I gave over seventy-five talks on Zoom and did live TV from my house. Every time I was on camera, I angled my webcam so high that I looked like a head in a box. I remember someone from *The Social* (a national Canadian daytime talk show) trying to get me to tilt my camera down. He was so patient, and I was so angry on the inside, needing to feel like his very reasonable request was outlandish so that I wouldn't have to have my chest made obvious to the world.

One morning in late 2020 I woke up and I couldn't move. Whenever I tried to lift my torso off the mattress, I had a searing pain that made me immediately stop trying. I had something close to a panic attack. Why? Because I saw myself being carried out of my house on a stretcher and my neighbors, delightfully nosey parkers all, gazing upon me in a T-shirt without my binder. *This*, not the pain and its unknown implications, is why I panicked.

My very nice partner suggested ibuprofen and a heating pad in case it was muscular. That helped, and after an hour I painfully sat up. What turned out to be a routine back spasm soon went away with my physio's help. What never went away, though, was the sheer terror I felt in imagining the public scrutiny as I was taken out to the (ultimately unnecessary) ambulance, with zero control over how my body looked.

The evidence compounded, and the organic decision made, I asked my family doctor to refer me to the local gender clinic and eventually had a seamless top surgery experience thanks to my trans elders' activism, as previously discussed. I had top surgery as a nonbinary person in a province where everything was paid for except my travel to the surgery center one province over. I even had Uber Eats vouchers for my recovery days in a paid-for Holiday Inn before my nipple graft bandages could be removed and I could head home.

The impact of my top surgery has been profound. I had it while teaching my classes online during the pandemic. Now that I'm back to large in-person lectures, I move my body expressively and all over the classroom. When I get hot, I take off my blazer. I actually don't think about my body at all, which is an incredible and unexpected gift from the trans gods.

The biggest difference, though, has been with my pronouns. Since my surgery, more and more strangers correct themselves and go with singular *they*, like my flat chest is just one more piece of the puzzle that leads folks in the right direction. Even more striking is my own response to being misgendered now. When people used to misgender me it would take the wind out of my sails. I would deflate and fold in on myself, even if a good-hearted person had made a simple mistake. But ever since my top surgery, when somebody misgenders me, I have to stifle a giggle! I don't always succeed, but I try.

I no longer feel like I am wrong, but that the mistake is theirs. I feel a deeply rooted sense of disbelief when I'm misgendered today because it has become so unbelievable to me that someone cannot see who I am. *I*, at last, see who I am. This is what top surgery and medical transition mean to me as a nonbinary transgender person: as someone who isn't a man and isn't a woman either.

All my trans life I've heard trans women and trans guys talk about how wonderful it is when your body more closely resembles the best and clearest picture of yourself that you carry around with you. But

I didn't know what a nonbinary body looks like. A nonbinary body is actually impossible to define because we look like so many different people—but knowing that top surgery could be for me would have saved me many years of discomfort and pain. And, it would have given me many more summer days outside in a T-shirt, or no shirt, like my secret not-girl self running around topless on a California beach when I was seven years old, joy incarnate.

I share my own medical transition story in a book on gender-friendly language and practice for a few reasons. First, I want my cisgender readers to feel your way into the depth of trans people's knowledge about our own bodies, even if we aren't yet able to act on that knowledge. You can't grasp the thought, time, and effort many transgender people devote to being who we are and not feel a sense of respect for what this entails. It's also important to know that transgender people experience transition differently, and that transition has many pathways and outcomes. As I have said in many places here, the goal of transitioning isn't always passing seamlessly as cisgender to others; it's more often getting one's own experience of the world and of one's body to better align with one's identity. Some trans people want to pass as cisgender men or women, and some don't. Some end up being able to pass, and some don't. And for many, like me, passing as "not *he* or *she*" is becoming a thing.

Lastly, a person who stands out to others because of their body, their gender expression, or how these work together is standing out *to others*. Standing out doesn't mean more than that. Standing out doesn't necessarily mean someone is transitioning, has transitioned, or will be transitioning. I've actually been congratulated by a well-intentioned stranger on "starting" my transition many years before I had top surgery, just because I have facial hair. Hopefully you now get why that person's remark was both funny and inaccurate. And standing out doesn't mean that someone isn't "really" their gender, which is assumed of some trans people in washrooms and other gendered spaces. Hopefully, knowing what you now know about transition, including what it is and isn't, you can explain why this is wrong.

Media Representations of Transgender People Are Changing over Time

When you say the word *transgender*, what do you think the people around you imagine? Of course, this depends on where you are and the people you're talking to, but also *when* you are. At one time in North America *transgender* meant nothing at all because it wasn't yet a word people used, even if there were transgender people in the sense of how we use the term today.

In the 1980s and 1990s, saying *transgender* or related terms probably conjured up talk shows like *The Jerry Springer Show* and *Donahue*, with sensational episode titles like "Mom, I'm Not Really a Boy!" These episodes often featured guests who had been assigned male at birth but didn't identify with or express their gender according to the rules of the boy/man category. People assigned female at birth but not playing by the girl/woman rules were far less visible. No matter what the daily topic was, these shows tended to dehumanize guests by positioning them as exotic creatures for the audience to feast their eyes on, unlike the "more discreet" ways we take our second looks when people stand out to us in real life (as discussed in Chapter 1). Because these shows encouraged open gawking, we can imagine how they affected trans people going about their day.

Today mainstream representations of transgender people are less sensationalized. There's a range of transgender experiences represented in popular culture, where for many years we were usually told only stories of violence and marginalization, like on crime shows where transgender people were represented as victims of violence. Trans people today are mostly shown in humanizing ways, going about the business of everyday life in broad daylight and with ordinary ups and downs. Think of Laverne Cox's character in *Orange Is the New Black*, or the trans characters who are played by trans actors (which hasn't always been a thing) on *Sense8*, *Transparent*, and *The Fosters*. And while Laverne Cox's character, Sophia, was incarcerated and therefore marginalized, she was a woman with a complex story and an important role in the prison community: presiding over the beauty salon.

The long-running reality competition show *RuPaul's Drag Race*, today with a dozen or more spin-offs across the world, has changed greatly in its treatment of transgender women over time. Love it or hate it, *Drag Race* has been a major vehicle of queer and trans public education since it began airing in 2009. The first transgender women to compete only came out *after* their seasons aired. When transgender women contestants began coming out *during* their seasons but before medically transitioning, RuPaul tweeted that a contestant taking hormone therapy would be like taking "performance-enhancing drugs" to compete in the Olympics. In the backlash that followed, RuPaul was excoriated by queens and fans alike for erasing the long history of transgender women drag queens and trans drag performers of all genders. And things have changed. Today, transgender women, like Kylie Sonique Love, have openly competed and won.

Since the first edition of this book, representations of nonbinary trans people have also exploded in popular culture, including named characters with *they/them* pronouns and secondary characters who very well could be nonbinary. The growing list includes Che Diaz on *And Just Like That*, Kai Bartley on *Grey's Anatomy*, and my personal fave: Adira Tal on *Star Trek: Discovery*. Even better, many nonbinary actors are playing nonbinary characters. The first nonbinary characters had to explain themselves or come out in a scene that awkwardly paused the plot, usually because they were misgendered and had to correct someone. But the current trend is characters just being nonbinary without an explainer: Their pronouns are used, and gendered terms are absent. This is what everyday nonbinary life is like, after all: going to work, getting a snack, saving lives in the operating room, saving the galaxy, and dating Miranda, not giving gender seminars (except me).

While these are all very positive developments, scholars like Julian Kevon Glover have argued that "humanizing" representations may

TWO-SPIRIT

Two-Spirit is a term used by some Indigenous people whose gender and/or sexuality don't follow the path of most others in their communities. *Two-Spirit* is a literal English translation of the Anishinaabemowin, or Ojibwe, term *niizh manidoowag* and was proposed by Indigenous people attending the Third Annual Intertribal Native American, First Nations, Gay and Lesbian American Conference held in Winnipeg, Manitoba, in 1990. *Two-Spirit* is often thought to be an add-Indigenous-and-stir substitute for other words in the 2SLGBTQIA+ acronym, which it isn't. Rather, *Two-Spirit* has a meaning both like and unlike words such as *queer* and *transgender*. One shouldn't presume that an Indigenous queer and/or transgender person necessarily uses it. Depending on many things, like a person's community ties and family histories, the term *Two-Spirit* might not be a good fit.

In Canada, for example, we often see *Two-Spirit* included alongside other terms in the acronym, and sometimes under the nonbinary umbrella. This is why it is included in this section, but I want to flag that there are Two-Spirit people who do identify with terms like *transgender*, *nonbinary*, and/or *queer*, and Two-Spirit people who don't. In March 2018, Joshua Whitehead, a "2SQ (Two-Spirit, queer Indigenous)" Oji-Cree author from Peguis First Nation (Treaty 1), was nominated for a Lambda Literary Award in the transgender poetry category but withdrew his book, *full-metal indigiqueer*, from consideration because he feels *trans* (the category in which he was nominated) is a settler term that doesn't reflect his Indigeneity. Whitehead's article on the reasons for this decision is essential reading, and is included in the bibliography.

reinforce rigid standards that are just plain unattainable for many trans people, and that many don't care about attaining in the first place. For example, Glover worries that Laverne Cox and Janet Mock, in particular—wealthy, body-size-normative, and cisgender-passing transgender women—may have come to "represent the narratives of all transgender women of color." Both Cox and Mock have also spoken out about their privilege. On the nonbinary side of things, I'll be watching for the diversification of mainstream nonbinary representations. Some, like Sara Ramirez's Che on *And Just Like That*, are people of color, but most are white. The preponderance of white *F-assigned* nonbinary people is also beginning to raise eyebrows in trans communities. I want to see more of my M-assigned nonbinary siblings on screen.

Beyond popular culture, transgender people are increasingly represented in electoral politics. In 2017, Danica Roem of Virginia became the first out transgender state representative in US history, with Sarah McBride of Delaware becoming the first out transgender state senator in 2020. And more keep coming: from twenty openly trans candidates running in the November 2017 elections to 2022's record fifty-five transgender people, twenty gender-nonconforming people, eighteen nonbinary people, and four Two-Spirit (see the sidebar) people running for public office. Canada is lagging a little at the federal and provincial or territorial levels, but local school boards are a different story. The elected chair of the Ottawa-Carleton District School Board in Canada's capital city is an out transgender woman, Lyra Evans, who also ran federally for the New Democratic Party in 2018. This is noteworthy because, following the US, Canada is beginning to see school trustee candidates emerge with virulently anti-trans platforms.

We Have Work to Do: The Range of Transgender People's Experiences

Regardless of all the ways that people's associations with the term *transgender* have changed and are changing, maybe helped along by pop culture and electoral shifts, today transgender people are still a marginalized population. Categorically, trans people are at greater risk than cisgender people for experiencing poverty, which has been linked to many factors, like leaving school early and having to leave a job due to persistent discrimination. You might be wondering how we square this circle: that transgender people remain a marginalized population but can also be Grammy-winning musicians, like Kim Petras, or have high-status jobs, like university professor (that's me). But I'm not a professor because I'm magical or because I work any harder than other trans people. As in other groups, transgender people just have wildly different life trajectories, health outcomes, and experiences of marginalization (including little or none at all) because of the diversity underneath the "T" umbrella, particularly in relation to race and socioeconomic status. We can generalize that being transgender means experiencing risk, but just because a person is transgender doesn't mean that person is necessarily at risk. Not all trans people face the same struggles.

The gender system is particularly deadly—and I mean that literally—for transgender women of color. For several years now violence against these women has been called an epidemic and a crisis. Writing in *The Advocate* in February 2015, noted trans author and activist Jen Richards voiced a now-common refrain in transgender communities: that the average lifespan of a transgender woman of color is just thirty-five years. From 2013 to 2021, the Human Rights Campaign documented 256 incidents of fatal violence against transgender people, and 85 percent of the people killed were transgender women. Sixty-six percent were Black transgender women. When it comes to reporting an experience of violence, the 2019 Trans PULSE Canada study found that only one-third of trans and nonbinary respondents believed police would treat them fairly. Many things cause the disparity among transgender people's life expectancies, and thus it might make little sense to speak collectively about "transgender people" at all when our access to life itself varies so widely.

In the face of such violence, you might feel like doing your gender-friendly best means very little. But this isn't true. The language and practices you'll learn in this book are a starting place for making the world safer for everyone who does gender (a.k.a. everyone alive and yet to come). For example, you know now that stranger violence against a transgender woman can begin with others perceiving her to stand out in a public women's bathroom and subsequently calling her into question. But if she didn't stand out, because the rules weren't as rigid and calling her into question just didn't make sense, the chain of events wouldn't lead to violence. If people around her read, understood, and recognized her as a woman with their words and their actions and stood up for who she was, maybe violence would be less likely. Small things add up. Language and practice aren't everything, but they aren't nothing either.

PART TWO.

WHAT TO SAY

The first part of this book laid out the landscape, rationale, and background information for making the shift toward more gender-friendly language and practices and why this is beneficial for everyone. Now I turn to what you can do, on a daily basis, to help bring about this shift where you are. A key domain of gender-friendly practice is language use: how we talk to and about other people around us. Why is language so important? Because we use words every day to refer to ourselves and others—not only gender pronouns, like *he/she*, but also other gendered terms, like *Sir/Madam*, *ladies/gentlemen*. We even do this during small talk when we apply gendered terms like *girlfriend*, *boyfriend*, *daughter*, *son*, *mommy*, and *daddy* without thinking. Our verbal participation in gender, as you saw in Chapter 1, often happens via words that we just don't hear ourselves saying anymore, but these same words can painfully stand out to others when they're used inaccurately. In the following chapters you'll learn—and unlearn—a lot about gendered language, starting with pronouns.

4.
A Gender-Neutral Pronoun Primer

WHAT Are Gender-Neutral Pronouns?

WHO Has Gender-Neutral Pronouns and WHY?

The HOW of Gender-Neutral Pronouns

This chapter is a deep dive into a key part of our language: pronouns. I cover who uses gender-neutral pronouns and why, provide an accessible introduction to singular *they* as a gender-neutral pronoun, and lead you through some hands-on exercises to help grow your fluency in its usage.

The general public's knowledge of and exposure to gender-neutral pronouns is increasing, in part because year over year, more and more transgender people are being who we are in all aspects of our lives. A second edition reader has probably met someone with *they/them* pronouns, which wasn't necessarily true when the first edition was published in 2018. In this primer, however, I'm going to begin at the beginning so that we're all on the same page. I begin with the WHAT of gender-neutral pronouns—which I'll refer to as GNPs from now on—followed by the WHO and the WHY, and then I explain the HOW: usage.

Because pronouns are a part of language, and gender-neutral pronouns are a part of a language change currently taking place in English, I've invited back the linguists who I interviewed in the first edition: Bronwyn Bjorkman and Lex Konnelly. Some answers remained the same, and some have changed because language is always changing. One thing, however, remains consistent: Gender-friendly language change isn't going away!

Bronwyn Bjorkman, PhD, is a faculty member and colleague of mine at Queen's University in Ontario, Canada. She studies formal aspects of language structure and meaning, what linguists call syntax and semantics. I met Bronwyn back home in Vancouver through a mutual friend when we were eleven years old.

Dr. Lex Konnelly studies language creativity and advocacy in trans, nonbinary, and gender-diverse communities. They now work as a research and development linguist in the tech industry, exploring the intersection of generative AI and sociolinguistics. I met Lex in the fall of 2016 when they helped me create resource materials for the No Big Deal Campaign (www.nbdcampaign.ca).

WHAT Are Gender-Neutral Pronouns?

Unlike *she* and *he*, gender-neutral pronouns are pronouns that don't position someone in either the M or F gender box. GNPs are invariably *third-person* pronouns: the ones we use to speak *about* someone else. For example, my own pronouns are *they/them*, but like everybody else, I refer to myself in the first person using *I, me, my, myself,* and you can talk to me in the second person using *you, your, yours, yourself.* Basically, all English pronouns are gender-neutral until we go to talk *about someone else.* So, the only pronouns that change when a person's pronouns are gender-neutral are the third-person ones.

Gender-neutral third-person pronouns can be divided into two groups, one far less common than the other:

- "Neo-pronouns," or new pronouns created especially for the purpose of referring to someone without using *she* or *he*.
- The second group isn't really a group at all, because it just contains *they/them* when used to refer to a single person.

LINGUIST Q+A:

Why Do We Apply Gender When We Apply a Pronoun?

Lex: The way that the English pronoun system works is that when we assign a pronoun to someone in the third person, we also assign them a gender category. Pronouns assign people to categories in many languages, but these aren't always about gender. Sometimes the categories are about things like prestige or social role. This is true in languages like Japanese or Thai, where you also mark the status of the person you're talking about relative to you.

Bronwyn: Some languages have pronouns that are just "me," "you," and "some other person" with no gender at all. Only about a third of the world's languages have gender pronouns. When you learn English as a baby, you learn that you have to put people in a gender box in order to refer to them. But this is just how English works at the moment. I can see English becoming a language that doesn't force you to socially categorize people if you want to talk about them. English could absolutely lose the distinction between *she* and *he* over time.

Lex: People are becoming more and more conscious that we assign a gender category when we use a pronoun. This is why gender-neutral pronouns are becoming more common, because recognition of how people live gender is changing. A language changes to address a need of its speakers.

WHO Has Gender-Neutral Pronouns and WHY?

A person has gender-neutral pronouns because these do a better job than either of the binary (*she* or *he*) pronouns in reflecting who that person is. It's safe to say that most people with gender-neutral pronouns fall under the transgender umbrella, likely on the nonbinary side of things. The online Gender Census that I referred to in Chapter 3, completed annually by thousands of people worldwide whose gender doesn't fit into the M-or-F binary, asks: "Supposing all pronouns were accepted by everyone without question and were easy to learn, which pronouns are you happy for people to use for you in English?" The wording is interesting. To my mind it reflects the fact that having your GNP used by others can be difficult, and that a respondent's authentic need can yield to sheer difficulty alone.

In 2023 the Gender Census listed thirteen pronoun options, including *he/him*, *she/her*, *they/them*, and a range of neo-pronouns,

 LINGUIST Q+A:

Why Is Singular *They* So Popular?

Bronwyn: All native English speakers have some uses of singular *they* already. One goes back to Middle English, which is saying "they" for a hypothetical person or for someone whose gender you don't know: "Someone's at the door. I wonder what they want." But *they* has been expanding for a few generations now, even outside of its usage as a nonbinary person's pronoun. Today some speakers fluently say "they" when they do know a person's binary (M or F) gender but it just isn't relevant to the conversation topic: "My friend's coming, too, but they're late." If you don't know my friend, gender doesn't matter.

Lex: Native English speakers are actually fluent users of singular *they*: "A new teacher has been hired at my school, and I'm excited to meet them!" It's already in our grammar. Some people use it only in limited instances, like for someone unknown to them. Others are what we linguists call "super-innovators" who accept singular *they* as grammatical in any circumstance, even when it's paired with a name they associate with a particular gender or a person they already know. Over time, it'll be interesting to see if more people become super-innovators, which I guess won't be as innovative anymore! In my opinion, we're already well on our way to that happening.

as well as "any," "avoid pronouns," "my pronouns vary," "change my pronouns frequently," and "questioning or unknown." Respondents could select as many options as they liked, and about *three-quarters* answered with *they/them*. Singular *they* is probably the most popular gender-neutral personal pronoun in English and an essential part of your gender-friendly language tool kit (I'll say more about this later on). For these reasons, singular *they* receives the most airtime in this chapter.

Regardless of singular *they*'s popularity, however, it's important to note that 11 percent of 2023 Gender Census respondents do not want to be called *they*. In 2023, the most dominant neo-pronoun package reported by these folks was *xe/xem* (pronounced "zee" and "zem"). And not all people who identify outside of the M/F binary have a GNP. Forty-two percent of respondents selected *he/him* and 32 percent selected *she/her*. A nonbinary (etc.) person might have *she* or *he* pronouns for many reasons, ranging from a mismatch of one's gender identity with current GNP options to being just plain fine with the one they were given to feeling daunted by the prospect of making a pronoun change, which today can still mean signing up for a lot of reminding and correcting.

A GNP Doesn't Have to Be Forever

Another reason someone might have a GNP—that I've heard exclusively applied to singular *they*—is that this pronoun can offer a space to catch your breath and figure out how gender works for you. Some people who take on singular *they* as a temporary breathing space are transgender. They know they need relief from everyday reminders of their assigned sex and gender category but don't yet know where they need to land. In November 2016, during a difficult Canadian conversation about GNPs sparked by an impending piece of federal human rights legislation, my friend Jake Pyne wrote a brave op-ed about this kind of singular *they* usage in *NOW Toronto*, a weekly independent newspaper. Today, Jake is an out transgender

MY PRONOUNS ARE NOT A "PREFERENCE"

We often hear people say "so and so *prefers* [pronouns]" or "what are your *preferred* pronouns?" Hearts are in the right place here, but I put scare quotes around "preference" language in the header because sometimes "preferred pronoun" discourse can minimize by saying that trans people's pronouns are like mustard on hot dogs or argyle socks. The best way to talk about someone's pronouns—including yours—is to just say "X *are* my pronouns" or "Y's pronouns *are they/them*."

I find it easier to explain why my pronoun isn't just a "preference" to someone who has also experienced pronouns as a negative force. Usually this is because someone has called him "she" if he's a boy or called her "he" if she's a girl. This can be incredibly hurtful and is just one more reminder that gender-friendliness benefits everyone. If the "big two" gender categories weren't so rigid, intact, and separate, they couldn't be used as weapons against anyone, whether transgender or cisgender.

man as well as a prominent researcher, educator, and activist on transgender issues. But from 1999 to 2001—long before it was commonly used for this purpose—Jake asked the people he worked with to refer to him using *they/them* instead of his assigned pronouns (*she/her*). "At the time," he writes, "I was certain I wasn't 'she,' but 'he' didn't seem right either. Being constantly gendered made daily life harder than it had to be, and it was already almost too hard. I had never heard anyone use the singular pronoun 'they' to describe themselves before, but it just made sense."

Another temporary use of singular *they* is gender-open parenting, where parents use *they/them* for their babies and toddlers until these kids can make their gender and pronouns known of their own volition (you can meet some of these folks via Tobin Ng's February 2023 feature on gender-open parenting in *Xtra Magazine*). This isn't an attempt to force children into being trans or nonbinary, which is impossible anyway (see the Chapter 1 sidebar on taking "nurture" too far). It's the opposite: *not* forcing children into any particular gender. As with the general population, the vast majority of children raised in a gender-open way will end up cisgender with *she/her* or *he/him* pronouns (the ones expected when they were born). But again, just like the general population, some won't. Either way, these kids learn a pretty cool lesson: that they know best who they are.

For most people with GNPs, our pronouns are a homecoming, not a place we move through. They express what we've known about ourselves over the course of our entire lives. However, it's clear from stories like Jake's and of kids raised gender-open that GNPs do other good and useful work in the world too.

 LINGUIST Q+A:

Is Singular *They* Grammatically Correct?

Lex and Bronwyn (at the same time): Yes.

Lee: That's decisive! How do you know that?

Bronwyn: Because people who are native speakers of English do it. That's how linguists determine whether something is "correct."

Lee: Do all English speakers have to use singular *they* for it to be considered correct?

Bronwyn: No. In fact, there isn't really one English. There are just people with languages, and some happen to be mutually understandable to each other as "English." Sometimes we socially index these differences, and sometimes we don't, like grouping people together because they say *ain't* or *y'all* or *about* or *aboot* and inferring where

continued on next page

continued from previous page

they come from. When the differences aren't socially indexed, though, we generally don't pick up on them. Even "Canadian English" is just an abstraction. So, we could never say "singular *they* is only grammatically correct if *all* English speakers do it," because there is no one English.

Lex: There is also a lot happening in languages other than English to accommodate nonbinary people and language, including in French, Italian, Spanish, German, and Russian. When linguists began studying nonbinary language, it used to be kind of a "gotcha" to say, "But if nonbinary people are real (etc.), why is this an English-only phenomenon?" Well, it isn't. In any language where grammar involves gender, this conversation is taking place.

Lee: So why do people think it's grammatically *in*correct?

Lex: In sociolinguistics, we differentiate between changes that are above and below the level of consciousness. If it's above, we recognize that it's happening and can comment on it. When social changes are happening, we often see that manifest in debates about "correct" language use. Singular *they* is at the intersection between grammatical change and social change. Grammar can't be separated from the social context in which it's used. The presence of nonbinary people in public life is increasing, and so we see resistance to the social aspect of that change sometimes appearing as a grammatical skirmish. Today, the social context has become so polarized that it can be hard to separate someone's actual grammatical struggles with singular *they* from their political beliefs about it.

Who Can Have GNPs?

I'll finish up this WHO and WHY discussion about gender-neutral pronouns by addressing a common question I received on my blog: Who can and who can't have gender-neutral pronouns?

People ask this question about themselves and about others. It's a funny question to be asked because it positions me as judge and jury on the matter. I perceive that people feel like they need to ask an authority (me, I suppose) if they don't feel "nonbinary enough" or "trans enough" to have gender-neutral pronouns, maybe because they have received these messages from other people under the "T" umbrella. This makes me sad, and I'll come back to this when I talk about public pronoun sharing (or pronoun "rituals") in Chapter 5. My own view has been consistent: A person has gender-neutral pronouns because GNPs are a better fit for them, and only they are in a position to know what fits. There's so much diversity among transgender people that we can't draw a boundary between who can and who can't. I've known people of many different stripes who have a variety of identity terms and understand their genders in many different ways, and who feel strongly that gender-neutral pronouns are a better fit for them.

That said, it's useful to keep in mind that people with GNPs who stand out (likely because they identify *and* are somehow visible as nonbinary or gender nonconforming) will have different experiences than those who do not stand out (likely because they pass as cisgender, no matter how they identify). For example, if you don't stand out, you can choose when to become visible as a transgender person and come out about your GNP. But as I noted about nonbinary outness and visibility in Chapter 3, invisibility carries its own risks, like isolation and misrecognition, even if it also offers safety sometimes. In fact, being nonbinary but invisibly so—whatever that means—could make it more difficult for others to understand and remember your pronouns. If you're interested, check out my interview with Morgan, a nonbinary person with *they/them* pronouns who is generally not "visible" like I am: https://theyismypronoun.wordpress.com/2016/10/18/we-are-they-episode-2-morgan.

The HOW of Gender-Neutral Pronouns

You now have an idea of WHY someone might have GNPs, and therefore also WHO tends to have them. In this section you'll learn HOW to say GNPs in everyday speech. I'll teach you how to consciously say singular *they* as a GNP, and include some examples of *xe/xem* usage given its status as the most common neo-pronoun in recent years. However, if you have someone in mind or at heart who has a different neo-pronoun, you can easily swap out *xe/xem* and use the tools in this section regardless.

XE VERSUS SHE AND HE

She	Xe	He
Her	Xem	Him
Her	Xyr	His
Hers	Xyrs	His
Herself	Xemself	Himself

HOW TO SAY XE/XEM PRONOUNS

Xe/Xem Pronoun	Xe/Xem Pronunciation
Xe	"Zee"
Xem	"Zem"
Xyr	"Zeer"
Xyrs	"Zeers"
Xemself	"Zemself"

As Bronwyn and Lex pointed out in one of the sidebars, singular *they* is already commonly used for referring to one person. For example, you would automatically say "FedEx came, but I don't know where they left the package." Of course, the entire FedEx corporation didn't show up and hide the package under the porch or leave it with your neighbor. Rather, *one* FedEx employee did, and we just don't know them or their gender: We can't automatically say *she/her* or *he/him* pronouns, so we automatically say *they/them* pronouns instead without thinking. This kind of singular *they*—for a person we don't know—is so common in Standard English that we usually don't realize it's been said. Next time you watch TV or listen to the radio, pay close attention. You'll likely hear *they* used for a single unknown or hypothetical person within the first five minutes or so. And it goes without saying that you've already said it yourself today.

However, using singular *they* as a gender-neutral personal pronoun means consciously saying "they" (etc.) to refer to someone who you do know. In fact, it means saying "they" because you know a pretty important thing about that person: that—odds are—they are under the nonbinary umbrella. For the most part, the only thing that changes with singular *they* as a GNP is how we're using a familiar part of the English language. But there is one exception to this rule. Have a look at the following table, and see if you can spot it.

SINGULAR *THEY* VERSUS *SHE* AND *HE*

She	He	They
Her	Him	Them
Her	His	Their
Hers	His	Theirs
Herself	Himself	Themself

What sticks out to most people is the word *themself,* increasingly said in place of *herself* or *himself* when talking about someone who uses singular *they.* Merriam-Webster notes that *themself* was the normal form for several centuries before 1450 or so and that more recent users include literary legends Emily Dickinson and F. Scott Fitzgerald. Today *themself* is seeing some resurgence and is included in the Merriam-Webster dictionary, albeit flagged as nonstandard. Although my ears are still learning, my brain thinks *themself* is better for referring to just one person.

Practicing with GNPs

The examples that follow contain a story about Evan, a fictional eleven-year-old who has GNPs and has a tough time at a friend's birthday party. We'll start with an example of Evan's story that uses *xe/xem/xyr* (pronounced "zee"/"zem"/"zeer") pronouns because these are singular like *she* and *he.* Learning to say a neo-pronoun means learning to substitute, for example, *xe* for *she* or *xemself* for *himself.* This isn't always true of singular *they,* which I'll come back to in a moment.

It's important that you read each example out loud. If you'd like to become more comfortable with saying GNPs in your everyday speech, it's vital that you practice by using your eyes, ears, and mouth simultaneously. This way you can feel your mouth forming the words while also hearing yourself say them and seeing them on the page. With this in mind, try reading the following *xe/xem* example a few times over.

XE/XEM EXAMPLE

On Sunday Evan was invited to the birthday party of a girl in xyr grade-six class. As a gift Evan brought something that xe had taken a great deal of time and effort to make xemself from found objects in the woods near xyr family home. The birthday girl openly rejected the "ugly" gift, and all of the other kids laughed at it before moving on to the next one. Evan asked to get picked up early, claiming that xe was feeling sick. At school on Monday Evan kept to xemself and avoided the other kids.

Now, using the table as a guide, translate Evan's story from *xe/xem* using pronouns from the singular *they* package in each blank space in the example. Remember to test your choices by reading them out loud, using your eyes, ears, mouth, and gut all together.

SINGULAR *THEY* VERSUS *SHE* AND *HE*

She	He	They
Her	Him	Them
Her	His	Their
Hers	His	Theirs
Herself	Himself	Themself

TRY ADDING SINGULAR *THEY* PRONOUNS

On Sunday Evan was invited to the birthday party of a girl in _____ grade-six class. As a gift Evan brought something that _____ had taken a great deal of time and effort to make _____ from found objects in the woods near _____ family home. The birthday girl openly rejected the "ugly" gift, and all of the other kids laughed at it before moving on to the next one. Evan asked to get picked up early, claiming that _____ was feeling sick. At school on Monday Evan kept to _____ and avoided the other kids.

If you did your homework and said your answers out loud, I'm confident that something stood out to you like a sore thumb: "Evan asked to get picked up early, claiming that they was feeling sick." This sounds wrong because it is wrong. Trust your ear and your gut, and remember that you already say *they* all the time when you don't know someone or their gender doesn't matter. If something feels really hard, it's likely wrong. For the most part, telling Evan's story with *they/them* (and not, say, *she* or *he*) requires simple substitution, but not always, because the verbs we use with *they* are always plural. Here are more examples where I shift between singular (using my name) and plural (my pronoun). In each example, *they* stands in for me just like my name does.

> Lee is coming over tonight.
> They are coming over tonight.

> The potato chip flavor Lee loves most is sour cream and onion.
> The potato chip flavor they love most is sour cream and onion.

> Lee wasn't home when I stopped by.
> They weren't home when I stopped by.

A quick tip for writing with singular *they* is to avoid mixing verb forms in the same sentence. Consider this example: "Lee is coming over tonight, and they are bringing the chips." This passes by quite easily to the ear when spoken but less so to the eye when it's written down. A better way to write this sentence, then, is to stick with my name: "Lee is coming over tonight and is bringing chips," or you could exercise your creativity and try any number of other things: "Lee is coming over tonight and bringing chips" or just "Lee is bringing the chips." There are so many clear and simple possibilities that you already know how to put into practice.

Before moving on I encourage you to practice some more by quizzing yourself using the fill-in-the-blank example you'll see next, and making up your own sentences about how Evan is doing in the aftermath of the birthday party using singular *they* or *xe/xem*. You can keep on talking to yourself or ask an obliging friend, partner, or family member to try it out with you in a conversation about Evan. If you know that GNP usage is something that people around you need help with, say, in your workplace, you can also organize some group practice sessions using the "Gender-Neutral Pronoun

Practice" discussion guide freely available on GenderYourGuide .com. Remember that it's okay to dissolve into giggles while you do your best. When I lead workshops, I welcome giggles during pronoun practice because it makes a new thing feel less scary and can be a lot of fun. I know people aren't laughing at gender-neutral pronouns or people who have them; laughter is simply how we dispel the nervousness we often feel about making mistakes.

Here are some conversation starters to get you going, on your own or with others:

- Why did Evan avoid other kids at school on Monday?
- What might make Evan feel better?
- What could Evan's teacher do about this?

QUIZ! FILL IN THE BLANK

On Sunday Evan was invited to the birthday party of a girl in ____ grade-six class. As a gift Evan brought something that ____ had taken a great deal of time and effort to make ____ from found objects in the woods near ____ family home. The birthday girl openly rejected the "ugly" gift, and all of the other kids laughed at it before moving on to the next one. Evan asked to get picked up early, claiming that ____ was feeling sick. At school on Monday Evan kept to ____ and avoided the other kids.

Advantages and Disadvantages of Different GNPs

Perhaps the main advantage of singular *they* is that everyone already says it, all the time, and we're familiar with its use. That leads to another advantage of singular *they*: that it allows for some blending in. My colleague was recently talking about me with her twelve-year-old granddaughter, who asked an excellent question: Why would I use singular *they* as my pronoun if it blends in? After all, if I feel good in my gender identity, and my pronoun expresses my gender identity, why wouldn't I want to use a pronoun that announces my gender loudly and proudly? My answer is this: As much as I love being nonbinary (which is what my pronoun means to me), on a tough or tired day it can be a blessing to be able to fly under the radar a little. Singular *they* very often goes unnoticed. People can refer to me, whether I'm there or not, without someone else picking up on a word they've never heard before (such as a neo-pronoun) and asking me all of the questions, however well intentioned.

 LINGUIST Q+A:
Let's Talk About *It*

Lee: I get a lot of questions about whether *it/its* is a gender-neutral pronoun someone can have. I have feelings about this, which I think I share with the people who ask me: It feels kind of dehumanizing. And yet, *it/its* is among the top five pronouns selected by 2023 Gender Census respondents! Help me out here.

Bronwyn: In English, *it* is used primarily for nonpersons, so I get how it can feel dehumanizing. But *it* is also used by some people to describe babies and pets, who are beloved non- or not-yet-persons. I'm an avid science fiction reader, and the genre now has fully developed main characters with *it/its* pronouns who are non*human* persons, but definitely persons, like in the Murderbot Diaries series, for example. There's a lot happening with *it/its* these days.

Lex: I think *it* might evoke difficult feelings for some of us who were gender-nonconforming kids because that word was used against us, or against different people precisely to dehumanize them for various reasons. Someone who has *it/its* pronouns might be saying they do not identify with the conventional human gender system, or they might be either reclaiming or playing with the dehumanizing aspect in some way. If you meet someone who has *it/its* pronouns, I encourage you to get curious about the source of your own discomfort, and be open to the fact that maybe it means something different for them.

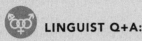 **LINGUIST Q+A:**

What Does the Future Hold for Gender-Neutral Pronouns?

Lee: When I interviewed you in 2018, some bold predictions emerged! One of them was about neo-pronouns: Either a consensus neo-pronoun would emerge, or neo-pronouns would fade as singular *they* became the consensus GNP. Is this what we're seeing?

Bronwyn: Not exactly. Singular *they* is still the most popular gender-neutral personal pronoun. However, behavior has shifted around pronouns and gender language needs more broadly. People can now access social scripts and conversation techniques for checking in about someone's pronouns. Sharing your own pronouns has become more standard. We might not need one consensus GNP because of this increased capacity to engage gendered language needs, whatever these are.

Lex: We also see more awareness that just saying the first pronoun that comes to you automatically for someone else isn't the best practice. Instead of getting consensus on "the right words people use," like some pronouns over other pronouns, we're seeing more consensus on "how to talk about the words people use." This is in many ways the best-case scenario because we're unlikely to get consensus on which words are right or accurate. Plus, it's very difficult to achieve consensus on particular words when a language change is in progress, especially one that has unfortunately become politicized.

Neo-pronouns have an advantage in that learning to use them means substituting singular pronouns (*she*, *her*, etc.) with other singular pronouns (*ze*, *hir*, etc.) with no other grammatical shifts. However, neo-pronouns also come with a disadvantage: They unavoidably stand out whenever they're used because relatively few people have ever heard these words before. This may be one reason why *they/them* is, year over year, the most common pronoun package favored by people who are nonbinary (etc.).

Singular *they* might be emerging as the dominant GNP, but it has its challenges too. A disadvantage of singular *they* is that it involves more than just substitution. As previously mentioned, if substitution was all that was needed, using my pronoun would sound like this: "Lee called to say that they is almost here." Rather, the following is correct: "Lee called to say that they *are* almost here." That's right: Singular *they* is singular in name only. Remember though, if something sounds funny (like "they is"), it's probably wrong.

5.

Strategies for Using People's Pronouns Correctly

Tips for Getting Pronouns Right, As Best As You Can

Comparing Two Common Pronoun Work-Arounds

How Do I Know? Ways of Finding Out Someone's Pronouns

What If I Do All These Things and Someone Still Gets Mad at Me?

Now that you have an understanding of what gender-neutral pronouns are and how to say them properly, it's time to go into a bit more depth about how to navigate gender pronouns in everyday speech given how gender is changing. I also address some work-arounds, or ways to avoid pronouns if you aren't sure what to do. I then offer a series of tips to help you make a pronoun change for someone you know, which double as tips for learning to use someone's pronoun when it doesn't feel like the one you'd automatically apply. There is also a section that shares strategies for finding out what people's pronouns are, whether in public gatherings or private conversations.

In the previous chapter I focused exclusively on gender-neutral pronouns. This is because they are one of the most obvious signs of how gender is changing and are a common way that people encounter the new gender culture firsthand. A major reason why gender-neutral pronouns are growing in prominence is because more and more people are identifying as nonbinary.

But pronouns aren't an issue only for nonbinary trans people. As you saw in Chapter 3, part of social transition for most, if not all, "binary" (M-to-F or F-to-M) trans people involves switching from one set of binary pronouns to the other: from *he/him/himself* to *she/her/herself* or vice versa. You also learned (in Chapter 3) that transition, whether social or medical, isn't the same for every trans person, and that "passing" as cisgender (in this case, as someone whose pronouns tend to be automatically inferred) isn't always possible or always desired.

And so, pronouns can also be an issue for transgender women or transgender men if they aren't automatically read by others as women or men, respectively. Here, misgendering (applying the wrong pronoun) can happen if a person's (visible) body and gender expression do not match stereotypical expectations for people of their gender identity. Unfortunately, misgendering is also a kind of question-calling, as are hostile, sarcastic, or exaggerated reactions to gentle corrections and reminders.

All this is to say that if you know someone before and during transition, you have to learn to do something new, even if this doesn't mean learning to use familiar words differently (*they/them*) or use likely unfamiliar words (neo-pronouns like *xe/xem*). Learning is still needed, and that means practice is probably needed too. But you might also need practice if you're meeting someone for the first time with *he/him* or *she/her* pronouns who doesn't quite line up with your own gendered expectations of men or women, respectively.

Tips for Getting Pronouns Right, As Best As You Can

Here are my best tips for changing pronouns for someone (whom I'll call "your friend"), learning to use someone's gender-neutral pronoun, or learning to apply a pronoun that doesn't come automatically to you. These are adapted from one of the all-time most popular posts on *They Is My Pronoun*.

Use Singular *They* All the Time
I often see people waiting until their singular *they/them*–using friend is around before they start rocking these pronouns, which

isn't a winning strategy. I think people do this because singular *they* doesn't feel new, but this is deceptive because it's doing something new, just with familiar words. When you're around people who aren't your friend, this is the perfect time to practice with singular *they* because it's already part of our everyday speech. It's unlikely anyone will even notice!

If you want to ease in, give yourself a challenge for one hour, during one meeting, or in the post-lunch lull, and use singular *they* for everybody. Strike up a conversation at the bus stop or at a tea party or wherever you feel comfortable. Of course, these challenges can also happen in a group, like friends or coworkers. If others *do* notice what you're doing, try to figure out why. What part of what you just said made them search for a gender indication and, finding none, really need to know?

Practice with a Friend

It's a great idea to practice out loud with someone else who also needs practice because talking is where misgendering happens the most. Meet up for a treat with someone you have in common with your friend and tell stories about them, doing your best to apply the correct pronouns. Reminisce about times spent together, or talk about things your friend might do in the future. This is an excellent opportunity to let off some steam and get giggly, which means you'll be more at ease when you make a mistake around your friend (which will happen, at first). Practicing with someone else can also help you become more comfortable with providing gentle corrections to others around you when they make mistakes. Trans people especially need you to do this when we're not there, so getting comfortable with correction is huge.

Take a Pause

Many honest pronoun mistakes happen when we go on autopilot: We're running through life and through conversations, trying to fill up empty space and time to banish the silence whenever it threatens. We tend to fear the pause.

But what if we reframed pauses, particularly in conversations, as opportunities? I'm not trying to claim that I invented mindfulness. Rather, I'm suggesting that practicing any mindfulness technique will help you with pronoun usage. You don't have to commit to a daily sitting meditation practice (although this can be helpful for many reasons). Start small: Try to remember to pause before you respond to someone, in any conversation, regardless of why. When we get caught up in the flow of a conversation, we can become automatons and fall back on our habits. This is where trouble lurks in the pronoun (and broader gendered language) department, where innate or familiar assumptions tend to rule the roost. The more you pause and become okay with pausing, instead of filling the space, the better you'll do.

Make Better Mistakes

Don't aim for no mistakes; aim for better mistakes. Mistakes are normal, not bad, when you're in the learning phase. There are only better mistakes and worse mistakes. A worse mistake happens when you misgender your friend and then lose your cool entirely. Mortified, you churn around in your own self-recrimination to the extent that your friend has to end up taking care of you.

If you feel flustered after a mistake, try your best to hold it together and make it a better mistake: Say a quick sorry, rephrase in a neutral tone, and move on. "Sorry—*they're* coming over later. And blah blah blah..." Sorry, rephrase, move on. Later, let it out in another direction: away from your friend. Go outside, go to the loo, get on your phone, and express your very real feelings of self-recrimination to somebody else (or write it down, if that works for you). A kid-friendly translation: Hold your flustered feelings like a pebble in your hand, put it in your pocket, and release it onto the ground next time you're outside.

The better mistake doesn't make our pronouns into a bigger deal than they really are, and it encourages us to offer you gentle correction when needed, instead of just sucking it up for fear of upsetting you. Which would you rather?

Offer Gentle Correction to Others

You do *not* have to wait to attain pronoun perfection to start offering gentle corrections to others. We are all in this together, so help others learn as you learn. Offering a gentle correction to someone looks like this: Make eye contact. Use a soft voice and maybe a gentle tap on the arm and say, "Remember, Lee uses *they*, not *she* or *he*," or neutrally rephrase what was said with the correct pronoun. Then move on. Sometimes the person might also need some positive reinforcement or a reminder that you, too, make mistakes sometimes. A gentle correction is the furthest thing from making it a big deal.

I'm going to give some tough love to people who have come to understand the difficulty of having a GNP sometimes, and who have begun to feel exasperated by others' honest mistakes. Thank you, with my whole heart, for your commitment to helping people like me move about more easily in this binary-obsessed world. But please do your best to keep your own exasperation away from the scene of a pronoun mistake, and away from the person who made it. I know you can feel our pain to some extent—and I say this without a trace of sarcasm, because you see and support us in working through the cumulative effects of standing out and/or being misgendered all the time—but forceful or exasperated corrections make our lives harder. They make our pronouns way too anxiety-provoking, and they risk sparking resentment among others who feel humiliated or called out for an honest mistake.

Be Real about Your Own Challenges

Take a second and make yourself remember a few times when you said the wrong pronoun for your friend and noticed (whether on your own at the time or later on, or because someone corrected you). What kind of situation was it, and what was your role? Were you leading or listening? Was it at the beginning (of a conversation or event), when things were getting started, or toward the middle, when you started to relax? We understandably want to run away from our mistakes or brush them off, and it's easy to feel annoyed with

AN EXPERIMENT:
TRY DITCHING ALL GENDER PRONOUNS

For a set amount of time, try referring to everyone around you without using any gender pronouns at all. How long can you go in a conversation? If you're feeling like a boss, can you go a whole day? You could also challenge yourself to notice and tally when other people use gender pronouns (or other words—see Chapter 6) for people they do not know, maybe even sharing your findings with those around you. This can help you build the mental muscles you need to gender people correctly and to start hearing others' mistakes, when they happen, so that you can help out.

ourselves or with our friend when awkwardness arises. Instead, I suggest practicing self-acceptance by leaning in to your mistakes and revisiting them later on. This way, you can identify and begin anticipating your own hurdles. You can begin to predict when you're most likely to get it wrong and try being a bit more mindful. What are some upcoming situations in your life where you need to refer consistently to your friend in the third person? Can you be extra nice to yourself, slow down, and practice in advance, whether that means pausing or trying out the other strategies in this section?

Embrace the Awkwardness

This is a theme spanning all of the tips I've shared so far. The reality is that having to notice your pronouns, correcting yourself, and being gently corrected by others is awkward. We fear the awkwardness, just like we fear the pause. Making a pronoun change or remembering to use an unlikely (to you) pronoun for someone is an opportunity to make friends with awkwardness—which is important because it's unavoidable.

LINGUIST Q+A:

Why Does Learning to Use Singular *They* Take Effort?

Bronwyn: Most of us are like second-language speakers when it comes to singular *they*. We didn't grow up using it this way as part of our dialect. But researchers have connected age with acceptance of singular *they*. The younger you are, the more comfortable you are. Knowing nonbinary people can also make it easier. Mistakes can happen more often when you're saying "they" for someone whose name you associate with *he* or *she*, as opposed to someone with a typically gender-neutral name. More generally, some people are just really good at languages, not just learning a new one but also even picking up a new accent, whereas others are bad at remembering names or learning new names that aren't part of their vocabulary. Some people say, "Oh, that's too hard. I'll just call you Bob." And others recognize that that's rude and work to learn the name and use it. Some are better at this kind of accommodation than others. But that doesn't mean you get to call someone Bob if that isn't their name. You'll make mistakes, but keep trying.

Lex: It's important not to demonize people who struggle to use singular *they* because the kernel of their struggle might actually be grammatical. There is something grammatical going on that is distinct from the social phenomenon. But it's not at all insurmountable. People can do this, and people do. People who want to use the right pronouns for someone else can adopt and come to use singular *they* with fluency. There are tons of linguistic changes that we participate in all the time without even thinking about it—don't be discouraged if it takes a few tries! My philosophy is that there are two chances to get it right: before and after you make a mistake. And a correction is just as good as not making a mistake.

Lee: So there's no linguistic argument to be made that a person "just can't use" singular *they*?

Bronwyn: No, but people have different starting places. Some English speakers are able to say *they* in conversation to refer to someone whose

continued on next page

continued from previous page

gender they do in fact know, but it isn't relevant. And some English speakers can't—yet—do this comfortably but always say "he" or "she" in these situations. Again, age can be a factor here. The good news is that practice can help. If you make an effort to begin intentionally saying *they* when gender doesn't matter, even for people you know, this can be a bridge to saying nonbinary *they* more easily. What's important is making pronouns something that you consciously apply.

Lex: Everyone can do it. It's okay if it takes some practice and feels a little unfamiliar to you at first. I have compassion for it feeling difficult, but it's possible to change with a little effort.

But being awkward isn't the worst thing ever, despite sometimes feeling that way. You don't have to make this look effortless because it isn't. Trans people are used to others trying their best and stumbling sometimes. We don't need you to be Meryl Streep about the whole thing. Try not to worry about seeming fake, preoccupied, or overly self-conscious while you're still in the process of working it out. I understand why people around me are kind of stilted or weird as they learn, and I know that this recedes over time. You won't become a gold-star pronoun champ overnight, and that's okay.

Celebrate Your Successes

The last tip I'll offer is to remember to celebrate your successes. Whether you met a solo practice goal, took an hour to get together and practice with someone else, made only X number of mistakes at the party last night, or got up the courage to gently correct someone, make sure to acknowledge your wins. Sometimes your friend might be so exhausted that they can't do this themself. I work hard at my own pronoun mindfulness practice: noticing and acknowledging the progress and wins of the people around me. But I don't expect that from other people with GNPs because not everyone has the resources that I do. Even and especially if your friend can't offer you positive feedback, you deserve it. In fact, if you don't take a moment to give yourself a high five and honor your efforts now and then, you might end up resenting your friend for not noticing, when they just can't. If you're a modest or particularly self-critical person, tell yourself that celebrating your wins is something you're doing for your friend, because it is.

Comparing Two Common Pronoun Work-Arounds

In an ideal situation everyone learns GNP usage at their own pace, subject to very realistic expectations, in a context where mistakes are destigmatized and accepted as part of the learning process. As you practice saying GNPs, you might be tempted to find ways to make things easier. That's not necessarily a bad thing. Two work-arounds I've seen people use are trying to avoid pronouns altogether by just saying someone's name and avoiding pronouns by restructuring your sentences a little. Let's take a closer look at each one.

Avoiding Pronouns

As you were practicing aloud in the previous chapter, you might have noticed that there are times when you do need to use pronouns and times when you don't. In fact, sometimes you can even avoid pronouns altogether. In my view, avoiding pronouns can sometimes be a strategy for affirming someone's gender by not misgendering them. Note that I said *sometimes*. I'm not giving my blessing to *complete* pronoun avoidance. Just like most people's *she/her* or *he/him* pronouns, my *they/them* pronouns say something important about who I am. They're not just words but an affirmation of my gender by the people around me. In highlighting pronoun avoidance as a work-around, I'm drawing on my own experience and, anecdotally, from speaking with other trans people over the years: that being referred to with your name or without pronouns can be better than being called the wrong pronouns.

If you find yourself in a situation where you're not yet confident about saying someone's pronouns correctly, there are things you can do that aren't ideal but are far better than misgendering them. What I've seen in many contexts is that, over time, people move through the learning process with gentle guidance from the person who has GNPs and—critically—from each other.

Avoiding pronouns because you don't want to misgender someone is one thing. But I've heard some people try to cope with pronoun anxiety or avoid it altogether by asserting that they'll "just say the name." This isn't a good plan. Read the next example out loud to see why.

THE "I'LL JUST SAY THE NAME" EXAMPLE

On Sunday Evan was invited to the birthday party of a girl in Evan's grade-six class. As a gift Evan brought something that Evan had taken a great deal of time and effort to make Evan's self from found objects in the woods near Evan's family home. The birthday girl openly rejected the "ugly" gift, and all of the other kids laughed at it before moving on to the next one. Evan asked to get picked up early, claiming that Evan was feeling sick. At school on Monday Evan kept to Evan's self and avoided the other kids.

Awkward, right? I'm being deliberately silly with "Evan's self" because, well, that just isn't something most Standard English speakers do. But silliness aside, I did this to make a point: Just saying the name instead doesn't actually make it easier to talk about a nonbinary (etc.) person when you have to.

In the next sidebar I offer another work-around: telling Evan's story without any gender pronouns at all. As you did before, read it out loud—perhaps after rereading the earlier *they/them* or *xe/xem* versions for contrast—and see if you can spot each change I made so that gender pronouns aren't required.

A PRONOUN-FREE EXAMPLE

On Sunday Evan was invited to the birthday party of a classmate. Evan had taken a great deal of time and effort to make a gift from found objects in the woods near Evan's family home. The birthday girl openly rejected this "ugly" gift, and all of the other kids laughed at it before moving on to the next one. Evan asked to get picked up early, claiming to feel sick. At school on Monday Evan avoided the other kids.

Restructuring Your Sentences

There are two things to take away from the comparison between the pronoun-free example and the "I'll just say the name" example. First, just saying the name is not a way out of the awkwardness that can come along with saying someone's GNPs or changing pronouns (at first). Saying GNPs is new for many and can feel awkward sometimes. A second takeaway is that it's possible to avoid pronouns by restructuring your sentences. Now try revisiting the prompts I gave you before, and see if you can manage to avoid pronouns when answering each one. I've given you a starting place, but I know you can come up with your own.

Why did Evan avoid other kids at school on Monday?
The other kids at a birthday party picked on Evan for bringing a homemade gift.

What might make Evan feel better?
Evan might feel better if a conversation happened with the other kids who were at the birthday party.

What could Evan's teacher do about this?
Evan's teacher could check in to see if a follow-up is needed.

How Do I Know? Ways of Finding Out Someone's Pronouns

In addition to the WHAT, WHY, WHO, and HOW, there are a few other things to know about navigating pronouns in the new gender culture. The idea that we can remain gender-language robots who don't have to think about the words we use for others is being gradually dismantled. This means you'll have to find out what another person's pronouns are instead of simply following your gut-level expectations if you aren't sure what to say. This has likely already happened to you. Finding out someone's pronouns can mean learning about them during a group share or go-round, asking them directly, or just paying attention and listening.

Asking and Answering, or "Pronoun Rituals"

Many people experience gender-neutral pronouns and even transgender people ourselves as a new thing, even if we're old news. Although the existence of transgender people has recently emerged into popular consciousness, many of the strategies in this book have been "just the way we do things" in trans-inclusive spaces for years. In these spaces there have evolved what I call "pronoun rituals," or familiar ways of asking about someone's pronouns and sharing your own.

By "ritual" I most certainly do not mean a dictate developed and adopted by an official committee. I just mean the kind of ordinary semiscripted encounter we have with others all the time, like asking someone for directions. A ritual is just a sequence of actions or statements with a proper order, time, place, and duration, where "proper" only means the way most others do it, such that this way doesn't stand out (a phrase that probably sounds familiar by now). In many faith traditions rituals have rules about how to participate, but also rules about who must, who may, and who may not participate. Holy Communion and bar or bat mitzvah have explicit (written-down) rules about these things, but most of our everyday rituals have implicit "rules" that aren't written down anywhere despite being strongly internalized and followed by everybody involved.

Let's think about the rules of the "asking for directions" ritual. Imagine yourself being the askee, or person being asked for directions by a total stranger. How are asker and askee supposed to behave? How long should the interaction last, and how far out of their way does the askee have to go in order to assist the asker? What "punishment" might be given to the asker or askee if they break the rules? Do boundaries exist around the interaction, or can it become something else, like conversation or flirtation? And how do we know if the boundaries are loosening or tightening up while we're still in the interaction? I'll bet you haven't thought about asking for directions as a ritual with implicit rules before, likely because you don't have to. This is just one of many rituals that you participate in without thinking. While asking and answering about someone's pronouns when you aren't sure can feel awkward right now, it'll likely become just as automatic as the many other rituals we observe with others as we go about our day.

Like the "rules" for asking a stranger for directions, the "rituals" for asking and answering about pronouns in trans-inclusive spaces have become less conscious over time. This is a good thing because it means that you aren't off on your own with no map when trying to find out others' pronouns. There are processes you can fall back on that already exist, and in this section I'll let you in on the "rules" so you don't have to worry about standing out. I think about pronoun rituals a great deal (shocking, I know), and I've come to distinguish between two kinds: more or less public and more or less private.

Asking and Answering Publicly

More or less public rituals tend to happen in group settings when people take turns introducing themselves with their pronouns and preferred name (because sometimes our legal name isn't what we'd like to be called, for many reasons). Public rituals usually happen regardless of whether anyone present is transgender. I say *more or less* public because "public" rituals don't usually happen in a fully public space, but in a space people have chosen to be in because of a class or a meeting: events where people are expected to interact with and talk about each other. Public pronoun rituals don't happen at concerts or restaurants where strangers aren't expected to interact.

More and more I see teachers or facilitators begin a class, meeting, or other participatory event by inviting those present to take turns sharing their pronouns (etc.) in a go-round. This has its advantages. It removes the necessity of people having to ask each other individually, and right away it cues participants into being more mindful with their pronoun use if, for example, someone shares their gender-neutral pronoun with the group. The go-round works really well for someone like me: an extrovert and an educator who is comfortably out and good at self-advocacy, and also as visible as a nonbinary person can be in this current moment (remembering what I said in Chapter 3 about the troubles with nonbinary visibility). As my mum likes to say, "I look like a they." It's not usually a big reveal when I state my pronoun, and people are even beginning to anticipate it. Hooray!

However, the go-round doesn't work well for everyone, often because of visibility issues. An anonymous gender-fluid person—I'll call them Y—once shared a story with me on my blog about a difficult experience with a pronoun go-round while they were passing as cisgender. Y uses both *they/them* and *she/her*. After sharing their pronouns, another person reprimanded Y for "co-opting" *they/them*, and this was because they read Y as cisgender. You know by now that I'm all about less and not more gender rigidity, and I'm disappointed that this happened to Y because it's clear that rigid and unhelpful rules about pronouns had become normal in this context: rules for who can and can't have gender-neutral pronouns. This, to me, is a problem, as is any rule so rigid that it can be used to wield power over another person.

Y's story highlights a key disadvantage of public pronoun rituals that have *rigid* rules for how people should participate, especially if participation is compulsory. We might think that compulsory sharing for everyone is good for transgender people, but it can be challenging if one isn't out as trans. This might mean a person passes as cisgender because of their transition or because they haven't begun transition (if that's their plan). Some newly identifying trans people just aren't ready to out themselves by sharing a pronoun that could jar with how others read them, a point well made by Elizabeth Reis, a CUNY professor of gender studies, in a *New York Times* editorial in 2016. Or you might not have it in you to educate the room about a gender identity like nonbinary (etc.) that many people still don't know about. Compulsory sharing can take away a trans person's freedom to choose when and to whom we come out, a decision often motivated by safety concerns.

While more or less public rituals tend to work well for trans people like me, and can be a powerful educational experience for cisgender people, the basic model needs renovation because of its risks for some others. Here are my tips for running a better go-round where you are:

- Have (preferred) name sharing be the stated purpose of the go-round, and explicitly make pronoun sharing an optional add-on.
- Conclude this name-only go-round by sharing your own pronouns (if you are comfortable doing this), followed by a clear invitation for anyone present to approach you about their pronouns if needed. Do your best not to look at anyone in particular while you say this. See the sidebar for more on sharing your own pronouns.
- Encourage but do not require people to include pronouns on a name tag or sign placed in front of them.
- Read the climate and the audience. What do you know about transgender people's experiences here? Are any trans people out? Have pronouns been shared here before? Do some homework as you consider whether it's a good idea to even

invite disclosure (see the second bullet). You learned about road-mapping the space around you in Chapter 2, but the best homework is listening to transgender people in your setting in order to learn about and be guided by *their* expertise. I'm sad to say that in some places, even inviting pronoun sharing could result in some people being called into question just because gender has become more scrutinized than it was before.

These tips put you in a leadership role: in charge of whether and how to run a pronoun go-round. Of course, this might not be the case. You might spend time in places where a pronoun go-round is unthinkable right now, as in the fourth bullet. But you might work in an office where compulsory sharing happens all the time as a matter of routine, or with an organization that indiscriminately includes compulsory sharing at its events, even if they move from place to place. If this is you, and you feel okay doing so, have a word with the person who makes decisions about these things and invite them to consider whether, for all of the reasons I've shared in this section, compulsory pronoun sharing is the most gender-friendly thing to do in your space(s). It might be, and it might not be. In my view it should not be automatically done everywhere all the time, and requires thinking and rethinking over time and across different contexts.

Asking and Answering Privately

More or less private rituals tend to happen in conversations when one person asks another for their pronouns. You might initiate a private ritual when someone's gender expression and/or what you perceive about their body don't firmly align with your expectations of people in the M box or the F box. I say *more or less* private because "private" rituals don't usually happen in total privacy. We generally don't lead someone down the hall and around the corner to ask them for their pronouns. That would be weird. Rather, the "private" ask happens during an ordinary conversation.

HOW TO SIGNPOST (SHARE YOUR PRONOUNS)

Pronoun signposting is a gender-friendly thing to do for two reasons. First, it widens the circle of people who know that pronouns are a thing to think about because they see or hear you signpost and want to find out why. Second, it lets people like (and unlike) me know that you're a person who probably gets it. When I see or hear someone signposting, I know that sharing my own pronouns with them will likely go okay, and that I can correct them if need be without it being a big deal. This is tremendously reassuring and, so far, I haven't been disappointed (fingers crossed).

Here's a good verbal signpost, or phrase you can say to share your pronouns out loud: "I'm [name] and my pronouns are [pronouns]." Try to avoid choice or preference language (see the sidebar in Chapter 4 for why). You can do this whether or not anyone else does it. Written signposts can be things like door signs, Zoom names, or name tags, whether there's a space for pronouns or you write them in yourself. You can also signpost in your email signature. Here's mine:

Lee Airton, PhD
Assistant Professor of Gender and Sexuality Studies in Education
Faculty of Education, Queen's University
511 Union Street
Kingston, Ontario, Canada K7M 5R7
lee.airton@queensu.ca | www.leeairton.com | @leeairton
pronouns: they/them
Queen's University is situated on traditional Anishinaabe and Haudenosaunee Territory.

Lastly, we can infer that a signposter is more likely to be gender friendly (and likely to know about and be broadly accepting of transgender people), but we can't infer that a person who doesn't signpost is *not*. Remember that everyone has their own reasons for doing it or not doing it. Only they know what's best for them. In my view, signposting, like public sharing, should never be compulsory.

Tips for Asking Privately

If you have made your best effort to read for someone's obvious intentional gender expression and you still aren't sure what pronoun to use, I suggest asking privately. If you need to know and reading doesn't help, private is best. Here are my tips for a successful "private" asking and answering ritual:

- Make eye contact, smile, and say in a friendly yet neutral tone, "Can I ask what your pronouns are?" The wording isn't as important as how you ask, as long as you avoid preference language. Keep the question light and open.

- When the person tells you their pronouns, respond with a neutral facial expression and body language as if to say that whatever they told you is exactly what you were expecting to hear. This is part of not telling people who they are without meaning to, a gender-friendly practice that I'll come back to in Chapter 7.

- After asking and receiving an answer, just say thanks and move along in the conversation.

- The nicest ask happens during a conversation when it becomes *necessary* to know my pronouns because, say, you need to talk about me right then and there. Maybe I said something you want to refer back to, like a comment about a restaurant I like that was just named anew in the conversation: "Lee was just saying that—can I ask what your pronouns are? [I answer.] Thanks. Lee was just saying that they really like that place too." This is nice because it's natural, and it flows with the conversation. That said, I'm happy for you to come over later on if you realized that you didn't think to ask when we were chatting before.

- Similarly, try to avoid coming up to me and asking out of the blue when we haven't really interacted. This can feel like you were trying to size me up the whole time from across the room. Maybe not, but it can feel that way, and that's not the greatest

THEY/HE, SHE/THEY, NO PRONOUNS PLEASE: WHAT DOES IT ALL MEAN?

By now, you may have seen "they/he," "she/they," or "no pronouns" in Zoom or an email signature. This makes sense. While 2023 Gender Census respondents—nonbinary (etc.) people worldwide—over thirty tended to select just one pronoun option, those under thirty tended to select two: most often a combo of *they* and either binary pronoun (*she* or *he*). "Avoid pronouns / use my name as my pronoun" was among the top five selected pronouns!

If someone has "flexible" pronouns (*they/he, she/they*, etc.), it's safe to read significance in the order. When I see *they/she*, for example, I infer that this person feels *they* is the best fit but is also comfortable with *she*. Here, I typically say *they* because making the effort to say a pronoun that—odds are—isn't the first one my gut selects is a gesture of care and respect. In my experience, however, the reverse (*she/they* and *he/they*) often indicates the person is happy to be referred to with singular *they* when it happens but is otherwise fine with the binary pronoun. That said, some under the trans umbrella would like their multiple pronouns to be used in a regular rotation as much as possible. TL;DR: It's okay to lean on the first pronoun, but it's caring and respectful to mix it up. Even better—if you find yourself getting to know this person, just ask: How would you like me to use your pronouns?

If you meet someone who would not like any pronouns used to refer to them, go back to my tips for avoiding pronouns, and remember that you can also speak directly to someone with *you/your* in most instances. For example, these are both gender-neutral: "Shane was just saying that!" and [turning to face Shane] "You were just saying the same thing!"

One of the things pronouns do, grammatically, is allow us not to say the same nouns (like names or jobs) over and over so that we can lower our cognitive load when speaking. If we're remembering to switch pronouns for someone, or trying to avoid pronouns altogether, this takes more effort than learning to say just one. That said, nonbinary Russian speakers are innovating in their highly gendered language precisely by switching between *he* and *she*! Once again, language is always changing.

feeling. Wait until it's obvious why you need to know, for practical purposes, and then ask.

- Another nice thing you can do as you become more comfortable is share your own pronouns with the people in your little chatting circle (standing around at a party, for example), and open up the space for others to share theirs, including the person/people whose pronouns you aren't sure about (but not while weirdly staring at them, which I probably don't need to say…but here we are).

My last word on asking for someone's pronouns will bring us full circle to the idea that this is a ritual. Rituals have unspoken rules that we can fall back on and that other people know how to participate in along with you. And rituals also vary from place to place. So, pay attention to how this plays out where you are, and see whether anything might modify the "rules" (tips, really) that I've shared with you here.

Some Risks of Asking Privately

There's a key difference between the kind of more or less public sharing that happens in pronoun go-rounds and the pronoun sharing that happens more or less privately in conversations. Public rituals tend to happen *regardless* of whether anyone present is transgender, but private rituals tend to happen *because* a person thinks that someone else might be transgender. In fact, directly asking a person about their pronouns can send a message that asking is needed because they look and/or sound like they are outside of the big two gender boxes. This can be a little dicey. It can make someone stand out even more or remind them yet again that they do. In some contexts I can even foresee someone using the pronoun question to harm someone else by calling them into question, maybe because they aren't doing gender quite like the other (for example) men or boys or women or girls around them. Many people, whether cisgender or transgender, work hard to be read as the women, girls, men, or boys they are, whether or not they're conscious of the work they put into it. A big part of why we express gender to others is to ensure that they use the right gendered language for us or accept our presence in particularly gendered spaces. For this reason, when I teach about gender expression, I say it's kind of like a sign that we each redraw every day and wave around at other people to help them get us right.

In the gender-friendly future I envision, the sheer "obviousness" of one's binary gender won't be as much of a badge of honor as it is today. Part of getting there together will be asking people about their pronouns and normalizing the pronoun question so that it isn't as dicey. But I also know that the pronoun question can be dicey now, and *this* is our starting place. The decision I choose to make—while not perfect—is to read for *obviously intentional masculine gender expression* as a sign that I should say *he/him* pronouns for someone, and to read for *obviously intentional feminine gender expression* as a sign that I should say *she/her* pronouns for someone. I say *gender expression* here because we generally have way more control over how we express gender than we do over our bodies and what they look like. Not every transgender person can get their body and others' perceptions to seamlessly align with who they are—with their gender identity—even with access to every available transition strategy.

For this reason, and particularly when I seek to do right by my fellow transgender people who, unlike me, are women or men, I choose to read gender expression, or the text that a person has most likely written of their own free will. I look for the presence *and* absence of gendered clothing, shoes, accessories, makeup, facial hair or eyebrow grooming, and done nails as well as hair length/cut/style. I read for walk, gesture, mannerism, and tone of voice, which are also part of gender expression. I didn't have to learn new things to read this way. I just had to recognize that I was already doing it all the time without thinking. And you can too.

Of course, there are reasons why reading for obviously intentional masculine or feminine gender expression won't work for some people. There are nonbinary people with gender-neutral pronouns and who appear to all the world like masculine men or feminine women. What's more, these folks might benefit from being asked about their pronouns, but they almost never are. As I've mentioned in other places, visibility is a trade-off. All this is to say that no strategy in this book comes with a foolproof guarantee for all situations. But if you read wrong and get corrected, you also now know how to make a good mistake: Say sorry, rephrase, move on. A starting place. In the next section, I'll share some other tips that don't involve directly asking at all.

Paying Attention and Listening

While there are all kinds of ways to find out someone's pronouns and avoid calling that person into question when you're just trying to get it right, *not* asking can sometimes be gender friendly. Even the best pronoun ritual—public or private—means an energy expenditure from a trans person. This is because sharing is sometimes still a vulnerable encounter where a trans person has to muster enough energy to make sure it goes okay and doesn't deter the asker from asking anyone else ever again. For this reason, there are things you can do to get it right that don't require any asking and answering at all, which can be nice. Here are some of them:

- Have a look at the person's social media accounts. There might be some activity or posts where their pronouns are shared, or there is other information you can use (think back to what I said about reading for obviously intentional gender expression). Instagram and X (formerly Twitter) feeds tend to be public, so start there.
- Social media can also help you find and learn from the person's close people. Look for friends in common who are active commenters, likers, or taggers, or who are in the person's recent photos, and see what pronouns and other gendered language they use for the person, if any.
- Listen to how other people who are close to this person describe them, and mirror that language. This works best when the close

people are choice family, close friends, or close colleagues. Our families of origin can struggle with name and pronoun changes and therefore may not be the best guide in all circumstances.

- Check in with one of their close people in person. You can ask directly, but you can also check in using open-ended questions instead—"How is [name] doing these days?"—and see what happens. Don't heavily probe in case the person has only private information that can't be shared.
- Open up a space for the person to step into. Find some time to sit down with them and check in, or invite them to join you in a meaningful activity. Share some space and time, and you might just be told in a gesture of trust.

What If I Do All These Things and Someone Still Gets Mad at Me?

First, I hear you. Thinking about pronouns and other uses of language (more to follow in Chapter 6) can feel like a lot of work before we get used to it and it becomes just another everyday ritual. You might do all the things I suggest and get a really difficult reaction from a transgender person when you're doing your very, very best. I'm of the mind that having gender-neutral pronouns or just being a transgender person (no matter your pronouns) is no free pass for hurtful behavior.

That said, transgender people face all kinds of challenges just going about our daily lives, and the everyday stresses of being a trans person can cause pent-up hurt to erupt onto someone who made an honest mistake. This is understandable. But to my eyes, that this is understandable doesn't make it okay. It's an occasion for repair of some kind, to whatever extent in whatever form possible. Sometimes repair can't happen, though, because that person just doesn't have the time, energy, or resources. That's unfortunate, but it also makes sense. It's a paradox: both understandable *and* not okay at the same time.

The best thing you can do with this paradox, if it happens to you, is to do your best to remember and internalize that *this is not about you*. Also try to remember that all you are doing to bring about a more gender-friendly world will hopefully make it less exhausting for everyone to be, express, and love their gender, including the person who just erupted onto you. And if this happens to you, try to do a nice thing for yourself in the name of self-care.

6.

Noticing and Changing Gendered Language

Pushing Out of Gendered Language

General Uses of Singular *They* in Work and Life

Alternatives to Common Gendered Language

This chapter is all about building your repertoire of general gender-friendly language practices beyond the basics of pronoun usage and navigation. You'll learn other uses of singular *they* that can benefit everyone, apart from using *they/them* when it is a particular person's pronoun. Next, I show how you can replace or avoid gendered terms we use all the time without thinking, first terms that indicate relationship (e.g., *brother, niece, girlfriend*) and then terms that indicate formality (e.g., *ladies, gentlemen*).

Pushing Out of Gendered Language

In Chapter 3, I joked that being a nonbinary person is kind of like being a gender wizard, but it can also feel like being a spy from the movies. Picture a James Bond–type breaking into a top-secret installation, lighting a cigarette, and blowing smoke to reveal the intricate web of laser beams that trigger the security alarm. The smoke here is a metaphor for all the ways I pick up on gender's otherwise invisible effects, learned from discovering lasers wherever I go and beginning to spot them in advance. Lights come on, sirens sound, and a nonevent becomes a situation, when all I did was walk into a restaurant, pick up the phone, or approach a customer service window.

When we need to refer to someone, we typically reach into our pronoun basket (e.g., *she/her* or *he/him*), honorific basket (e.g., *Mr.*, *Ms.*, or *Mrs.*), and salutation basket (e.g., *ladies* and/or *gentlemen*, *ma'am* and/or *sir*). My gender expression and body combination means that people often have to think a little bit more about which pronouns, honorifics, and salutations to use for me, and they tend to notice themselves noticing that they have to make an effort at something that's usually automatic. Those efforts usually yield the same result: I get misgendered and called "she" or "he." In recent years, I'm happy to report that this is happening less and less, to me and in the places I spend time. More and more folks see me and say "they" or avoid gendered pronouns altogether. That doesn't mean all trans people are being gendered correctly, but I think it does mean that, on the whole, people are increasingly noticing themselves noticing, and saying something else. However, as gender diversity becomes a more polarizing topic even though trans people generally want to live our lives in peace, some may notice themselves noticing and intentionally choose to misgender someone. This hurts much more than a casual mistake and is often accompanied by threats—implied or explicit—of harassment or violence if we don't just go away quietly.

Back to automatic—not intentional—misgendering. I can be just as much of a gender language robot as anybody else. But knowing that automatic gendering doesn't work for everyone, I've developed some strategies for shifting my language even when my gut is firmly trying to make me say words from one side of the binary. In this section I'll share three of these practices:

1. Using singular *they* as a general gender-friendly practice
2. Building your vocabulary of alternatives to familiar gendered terms
3. Learning to avoid telling people who they are (or should be) without thinking

General Uses of Singular *They* in Work and Life

If you did your homework in Chapter 4, you're on your way with singular *they*: with using "they are" (etc.) to refer to a single person. This is a good thing to do when it's someone's own pronoun, but that's not the end of the road for singular *they* as a tool in your gender-friendly kit. As you learned from my linguist friends Bronwyn and Lex, each of us is a pro at saying "they" for a stranger whose gender we don't know, and we do it every day without anyone noticing, ourselves included. In fact, because it's already natural for native English speakers, you can begin to intentionally use singular *they* all the time without confusing the people you're talking to.

Using Singular *They* When You're Unsure

Let's look at an example: my doctor's receptionist needing to ask the doctor a question about my care. While we're in second-person (*you/your*) territory—where the receptionist is speaking *to* me—the risk of misgendering is very low. But with the shift to third person—where the receptionist is speaking *about* me to the doctor—we're in the misgendering red zone. Suddenly pronouns come into play. My androgynous gender expression, gender-neutral name, gender-neutral *Dr.* title on my patient file, and the lack of any sex marker on my Ontario health card (standard on the latest version) aren't helping the receptionist decide what to say. This is where a more general use of singular *they* would be helpful. Instead, however, most people in this situation just choose a (wrong) binary pronoun (*he* or *she*). I usually offer a gentle correction in these situations (and in most other situations too) because I'm an educator, and because I know I'm not the last person who'll need this individual to notice and change how they use gendered language. But wouldn't it be lovely if I didn't have to?

Using singular *they* as a gender-friendly practice means acting on a few things you've learned in this book so far:

- Your basis for "knowing" someone's gender and automatically applying *she/her* or *he/him* pronouns isn't always reliable.
- Misgendering someone is just one more way of calling them into question, whether you mean to or not.

You now know a little bit more about transgender people and how we're often called into question—sometimes with horrible consequences—because our gender expressions and/or our bodies aren't thought to line up with expectations for people in the male/boy/man box or the female/girl/woman box. You know that some trans people choose or are able to "pass" seamlessly as cisgender men or women, and that some trans people choose not to or can't. You also know that some transgender people are nonbinary, like me, and that there isn't just one way to "look like" a nonbinary person.

All this is to say that the truth of someone's gender identity doesn't lie in whether a perfect stranger can mindlessly tick one of the binary boxes based on how that person looks or sounds. What you think you know about someone else on the basis of what you see or hear might not actually reflect who they are. When you presume otherwise, you welcome only some people into your space: people who are or who seamlessly pass as cisgender. But when you understand that what you see or hear might not be the whole story of a person's gender, you can make more gender-friendly choices that work for everyone.

If singular *they* is used for everybody who walks into, say, your office, and if people see this happen for everybody, then you can't make a particular person stand out. The challenge is that the more we think we "know" about a person's gender—which, in person, includes what we see *and* what we hear—the harder it is to remember that our "knowledge" is unreliable. And so, you'll be most successful in making the shift to general singular *they* usage if you do it with others in your life, perhaps with some help from Chapter 4. For example, a doctor's office could make it a policy to use singular *they* for patients or to look at a patient's file before using any gender pronouns. This last suggestion would work best if the office's electronic records software had a pronoun box that just got filled in as part of patient intake.

Overall, any effort that you devote to not misgendering trans people, including general singular *they* usage, stands to benefit others too. You don't have to be trans to be misgendered, and trans people aren't alone in getting hurt when it happens. For example, there are cisgender men and women whose voices don't line up with expectations for "how men should sound" or "how women should sound." Another example is names. We commonly come across culturally unfamiliar (to us) names and can't tell if they're gendered. Using singular *they* can be a good strategy here, too, as it very often goes completely unnoticed.

 THE BENEFITS OF ASKING EVERYONE

Service Canada, the customer service arm of the federal government, has guidelines surrounding gender-friendly language. (A person would call or walk into a Service Canada storefront to do things like apply for employment insurance if they've been laid off or access their federal public pension.) Service Canada employees have been asked to avoid using gendered language (*madam, sir, Ms., Mr.*) until they've asked how a client likes to be addressed.

This has stirred up debate, likely provoked by a confusing rollout. Some critics have even called the guideline a waste of employees' time and of public money that should be spent elsewhere. I can see why people would think this if they aren't used to being called into question by others. If you haven't felt this every day or every time you step outside of your house, you might not (yet!) be able to understand. But from where I sit, there's no harm whatsoever in everyone being asked how they'd like to be addressed. With this three-second interaction, the vital services rendered by Service Canada become accessible to everyone, gender-wise.

Implementing Singular *They* in a Workplace

Even if a gender-neutral pronoun or other language policy is impossible where you work, you can make the decision on your own to use singular *they* as a rule for people, whether in person or on the phone. This probably means some practice, using some of the exercises and strategies I included in Chapter 4. Another option for short-term interactions is to avoid using pronouns at all. In the following table I give some suggestions for how a doctor's office receptionist could talk about a patient, first using singular *they*, and then avoiding gender pronouns altogether. Both can be readily adapted to other contexts. Just like you did in Chapter 4, try reading each example out loud.

GENDER-FRIENDLY WAYS OF TALKING ABOUT A CLIENT OR PATIENT

Less Gender Friendly	More Gender Friendly
He wants to know if he's able to get a prescription refill.	They want to know if they're able to get a prescription refill. The patient is asking about a prescription refill.
Can she decide herself when to take off the bandage?	Can they decide themself when to take off the bandage? Can the patient decide when to take off the bandage?
When does he need to come back for a follow-up?	When do they need to come back for a follow-up? How long after a [procedure] before a follow-up is needed?

Let's take my doctor's office example and move it onto the phone, as if I'd called to make an appointment or ask questions about my prescription. On the phone the receptionist has no gender information to go on other than my voice, which is higher in pitch than the average "man's voice" and about average for a "woman's voice," whatever that means. From the sound of my voice alone, then, the receptionist unconsciously "knows" my gender and likely selects *she/her* pronouns. And voilà: I am misgendered based on my vocal pitch.

In Chapter 5, I suggested reading a person's *obviously intentional* gender expression in order to infer their pronouns. Each person's gender expression is kind of like a sign that tells others how to appropriately refer to and interact with them. Many people—whether trans or not—devote a lot of time and energy to being highly readable as men or as women, and if someone is very obviously putting out gender expression signals that X is their gender identity, reading these signals can be a gender-friendly practice. Your voice is part of your gender expression, whether you're aware of it or not. You learned in Chapter 3 that vocal training can be part of social transition for some transgender people, and that training can involve changing pitch but more easily targets tone and inflection. All this is to say that if you hear someone speaking on the phone with what—to you—sounds like a "man's voice" in terms of pitch but their tone and inflection sound like "how women talk" in your local context, you might choose to read this obviously intentional gender expression and use *she/her* pronouns, *Ms.*, etc. However, if you're unsure, using singular *they* to refer to someone who's on the phone is a better idea than just being a gender-language robot. And remember, if you get it wrong, you now know how to make a good mistake: Say sorry, rephrase, and move on, all in a neutral manner.

Avoiding Gendered Terms and Titles

Any office can adopt a policy that walk-ins are not to be referred to with gendered terms, titles, or pronouns. Here are some gender-neutral alternatives to statements commonly used in frontline office settings.

GENDER-FRIENDLY OFFICE GREETINGS

Less Gender Friendly	More Gender Friendly
There's a lady here to see you.	There's someone here to see you. Your twelve o'clock appointment has arrived. Are you ready for me to send in your visitor?
Can I get your name, Mr....?	Can I ask your name? Whom should I say is waiting?
This gentleman needs assistance.	I have someone who needs assistance. Do you have a moment to assist someone?

Alternatives to Common Gendered Language

When you realize that gender is more complicated than a quick, unconscious inference based only on what you can see or hear, it becomes apparent pretty fast that gender is everywhere in our vocabulary and not only in our grammar. And so, another gender-friendly practice is learning to replace some of the most automatically applied words in your lexicon. In this section I'll explore some alternatives and how to use them, beginning with language that indicates relationship, followed by language that indicates formality.

Gender-Neutral Language That Indicates Relationship

In the next table, you'll see common gendered terms that indicate relationship and some emerging gender-neutral alternatives. Some alternatives are more obvious and self-evident than others, but they all have their uses depending on who's using them and the context of their use.

ALTERNATIVES TO COMMON (GENDERED) RELATIONSHIP TERMS

Instead of only saying...	...you can also say:
Husband, wife	Spouse, partner
Girlfriend, boyfriend	Partner, lover, sweetheart, sweetie, date, significant other, main squeeze, "person X is seeing/dating," person (with possessive: my, his, her, their, hir, etc.)
Girl, dude, guy (as a form of address, like "Hey, girl")	Friend, pal, chum, dear, love, champ, kiddo, captain
Daughter, son	Kid, child, baby, "our/my eldest," "our/my youngest," "our baby"
Granddaughter, grandson	Grandchild, grandkid
Sister, brother	Sibling, sib
Aunt, uncle	"My dad's sibling," "my mum's sibling," untie
Niece, nephew	"My sibling's kid," nibling, sibkid
Mother/mum/mummy/etc. or father/dad/daddy/etc.	Parent
Grandmother, grandfather, etc.	Grandparent

Adding the right-hand terms to your gender-friendly tool kit is useful for a few reasons. First, they are handy in situations where you know a person is nonbinary and you need to talk about their relationship to others. Second, these terms are helpful when you want to avoid imposing a gender ("Take this home to your mummy") or the entire gender binary *and* heterosexuality ("Take this home to your mummy and daddy") just because you need to say something.

Many terms in the table are geared toward situations where you're speaking about someone else's parent, sibling, kid, etc., and this is why I have only *parent* and *grandparent* up there: because these are terms that you can use to indicate *other* people's relationships. Of course, people get called all kinds of wonderfully unique gender-neutral terms by their *own* kids or grandkids. I know many parents who get called their names or a mangled version made up by their own kids while developing language. This is also true for people under the transgender umbrella. The term *baba* has gained in popularity among trans parents and queer parents alike, and I have also heard people use *abba, zaza,* or *roo*. "Roo" is adorably short for *kangaroo, referring to the parent who carried the child before birth,* regardless of the parent's gender. These lesser-known terms can be replaced by *parent* in less personal talk.

Of course, the creativity doesn't stop at parent alternatives. My brother often calls me "sib" as a term of endearment, and my sister sometimes calls me "dingus" (which has nothing to do with gender, but I find it hilarious, so it's included here). My brother's grown-up kids sometimes refer to me as their "untie" instead of *uncle* or *aunt,* but both called me Wizzie when they were little, a word the older one came up with as a toddler. As a result, my sister's young twins have grown up calling me Wizzie because that's the word my family created for me, for this purpose. And it continues! Today, my friends Megan and Zach have twin toddlers, and because they are part of my choice family, these babies know me as their Wizzie too.

I've noticed *sib* and *untie* floating around online and in conversation, as well as words like *nibling* and *sibkid* in place of *niece* and *nephew*. *Untie, nibling,* and *sibkid* stand out, however, and sometimes it might be best to use the phrases in the table instead ("my sibling's kid"), particularly when you're speaking with people who you don't know very well. You'll probably get some blank stares until

MY DAD WAS A FUNNY GUY, OR FINDING YOUR OWN WAY

Throughout our lives, when my siblings or I would come downstairs in the morning, my dad would sing the Miss America theme song to announce our presence, especially when we'd slept way in and looked like it. We're Canadian, but that didn't seem to matter one bit. When I came out as nonbinary, my dad—a funny guy—wasted no time in adapting his favorite joke. He greeted me in the morning by singing, "There they are, Person America!" I rolled my eyes, he laughed like the daddest dad ever, and he gave me a great big hug. My dad also sometimes introduced me as his "offspring," which could stand out but gelled with his jokey personality. All this is to say that our personalities and relationships play into how we come to do gender right for the people we love. If you or someone you love is nonbinary, for example, you can work together to find your own way forward, and just try something out and see how it sits.

these terms become normalized, but normalization is well underway. At the time of writing, "nibling" was one of Merriam-Webster's "Words We're Watching."

Helping Trans Kids Think Through and Stand Up For Their Gender-Language Needs

After many years of being out as nonbinary, I have a strong knowledge of which words work for me. But if you're the parent (or other significant adult) of a trans kid, particularly one who is newly coming into themself, it might be a good idea to sit down and have a practical conversation about what terms work for them. They might need some support in thinking about what it looks like to meet those needs when you're all visiting the grandparents, or when you're wandering about in the world without them and run into somebody you haven't seen for years.

It can be helpful to "interview" the kid and help them think through terms they feel comfortable with, as well as when and where to use them. When you run into Linda from church at the corner store, for example, do you have to use the new terms and bring on all of the questions even if your kid has moved away and might never see her again? The clearer and more actionable your kid's needs are, and the more positive, collaborative communication you've had together about them, the more likely you will be to enjoy your relationship. Here's I've included a tool to help guide this "interview" with your kid about their needs. Of course, this can support any other situation in which you're collaborating with someone on having their gender needs met in a context you share. Many of these questions prioritize safety and how this changes among the various contexts of a trans person's life.

WHAT
- What term(s) can people use to describe you and your gender to others?
- What terms can your family members use for you that indicate your relationship?
- What term(s) can your partner(s) use for you that indicate your relationship, or what term(s) can people use to describe your relationship?

WHERE
- Places where you need people (or a particular person) to *always* work to use your pronoun, preferred name, or correct gender terms:
- Places where you need people (or a particular person) to *never* use your pronoun, preferred name, or correct gender terms:
- Places where people (or a particular person) can use their judgment:

WHO

- People whom you need people (or a particular person) to *always* remind/correct about your pronoun, preferred name, or correct gender terms:
- People whom you need people (or a particular person) to *never* remind/correct about your pronoun, correct name, or preferred gender terms:
- People with whom people (or a particular person) can use their judgment:

In Chapter 8, I talk about how to put this information to use.

Gender-Neutral Language That Indicates Formality

Gender doesn't show up only in the terms that indicate our intimate, personal, or family relationships. Gender also shows up in formal language, including terms—*sir, madam, ma'am, ladies,* and *gentlemen*—and titles—*Mr., Ms., Mrs.,* and *Mx.* (see the sidebar).

There are some situations in which gendered terms are particularly ingrained. I love food, both cooking and enjoying, and a special treat for me is going to a fancy restaurant for dinner once in a while. I'm that person who reads everything on the menu and asks a lot of questions. The problem with this hobby—well, the problem most relevant to this chapter—is that the fancier a place or situation, the more likely it is that gendered language will be used there.

Formality in Oral Language

In the North American service industry, formality is gendered. In high-end service contexts, we seem to think that the only way to show deference and respect to customers is by declaring how obvious it is that they are ladies and/or gentlemen, whether by saying these terms or saying "sir" or "madam." This formal-equals-gendered mentality is a hangover from when restaurant culture was far more gendered in every way. *New York Times* writer Frank Bruni reminds us that women used to receive menus and have their plates cleared before men, and that some restaurant software even let servers punch in "L" for lady! Even today, when these habits have receded, as a nonbinary foodie I find myself going back to the same local cafes and

 A GENDER-NEUTRAL HONORIFIC: MX.

Mx.—often pronounced "Mix" and sometimes "Mux"—is a gender-neutral alternative to Ms., Mrs., or Mr. If I weren't Dr. Airton, I'd be Mx. Airton. Mx. was added to the Merriam-Webster dictionary in 2017, although the dictionary's blog says the term first appeared in print in 1977. Today, Mx. is commonly offered as an option on forms of all kinds, including by major banks, airlines, and postsecondary institutions. Merriam-Webster notes that Ms. had an eighty-five-year gap between being coined in 1901 and being adopted in 1986 by The New York Times, whereas Mx. was added to the dictionary only forty years after being coined. Things may be speeding up! That said, the 2023 Gender Census found that fewer than one in five respondents (people who do not fit into either the M or F binary boxes) preferred Mx., with over 40 percent preferring no title at all.

In traditionally organized companies, partners and leaders are often called Ms. or Mr. so-and-so even when everyone else is referred to by their first names. If workplaces become less hierarchal, perhaps honorifics will fade away. Schools are another setting where honorifics are hierarchal, marking the difference between teachers (with) and students (without, except when someone is in big trouble). As a person who teaches people to be teachers in a university, I know that more and more young transgender people are finally having a good enough experience of school that they want to go back and be teachers. In Canada, a nonbinary teacher using a title of Mx. is their human right on the grounds of gender identity and gender expression. However, because Mx. is still new, even in Canadian schools some choose to go by a title—"Teacher [Last Name]"—or just by their last name, period. This works unless your last name is also a first name, like Stewart, James, or, well, Lee!

restaurants in Kingston where the food is delicious and, just as importantly, the staff have gotten to know me. You might call this a gender-friendly self-care practice.

Formal gendered language is common at the other end of the customer service spectrum, too, like when you're lining up to get a refund at Target or calling a customer service number to complain about your Internet service. Maybe calling someone "ma'am" or "sir" in lukewarm tones is thought to insulate a customer service representative from the rage and pain of someone whose fifth air mattress is leaking, or whose Internet isn't streaming Netflix fast enough. Whatever the reason, as soon as a representative hears my voice on the phone, it's usually "ma'am" to the max. Once they've pulled up my account, even though my name is gender-neutral and my title is Dr., I'm *still* unthinkingly called "miss" or even "missus." Of course, I'm not alone. I like to joke that I got my PhD so I could liberally sprinkle *Dr.* all over my bills and plane tickets, which sometimes works to cue someone into changing their use of formal gendered terms.

Very often people who work in the service industry ask me what they can say instead of terms like *ladies, gentlemen, sir,* and *madam.* I draw their attention to other ways we show formality other than gendering people. Imagine a server sauntering over to a table and mumbling "Hello, ladies" with a flat affect, arms crossed, and zero eye contact. Now imagine the same server walking over and, with a slight incline to their body, saying "Good evening" while making brief eye contact with everyone seated around the table. Which is more formal? My partner and I recently went to a fancy restaurant with a visiting friend, and we were kind of surprised when the waiter pulled out the fourth chair and plopped down to describe the daily menu features and take our order. While it didn't bother me and I was happy to chat, it reminded me that there are conventions for showing formality, and these often have nothing to do with language at all, let alone with gendered language. In addition to "Good evening," other helpful gender-neutral phrases you can use to convey

"INSTEAD OF SAYING LADIES..."

In 2015 Vancouver-based artist Toni Latour and collaborator Jenny Lynn released a business card–sized intervention for diners to leave on the table, particularly targeting the indiscriminate use of *ladies* that irritates many people, whether trans or no. On the cards, Latour and Lynn suggest gender-neutral replacements for *ladies* or *gentlemen*, like *friends*, *folks*, and *everyone*. Like I do in this book, they also warmly invite the server to "join the movement to be more mindful of language!" You can learn more and print your own cards at www.tonilatour.com/hello-there.

respect (in combination with body language, eye contact, and tone) include:

- Welcome to [restaurant].
- May I help the next guest?
- And for you?
- What will you be having?
- How is everything tasting?

I'm sure you can think of many more, including adaptations of this approach across contexts. How could this kind of gender-free formality be useful in places where you work or spend time?

Formality in Written Language

So far, I've focused on how to navigate gender when you're *speaking* in a formal context, but there are also things to know about gender in formal *writing*. I'm often asked how to avoid "Dear Sir or Madam..." or "Dear Mr. or Ms. [name]..." in correspondence. Unlike with general singular *they* usage, I don't suggest using *Mx.* for people you don't know because *Mx.* isn't yet common in English. I also want to hold space for all the people who like their gendered honorific of

Mr., Ms., or *Mrs.,* whether they are cisgender or transgender. After all, I know how much I love my own. And I'm very okay with being respectfully asked, particularly if everyone else is too. An increasingly common alternative is using a person's full name instead: "Dear Lee Airton..." This is more formal than addressing someone by their first name alone, and doesn't require gendering.

Changing how honorifics are used in correspondence can bring on a headache, however. Organizations often use templates for mass correspondence via email or in print, and these tend to generate gender-*un*friendly outcomes like that old chestnut "Dear Sir or Madam." Removing honorifics or shifting to full names could mean changing a proprietary software program, a problem that many colleges and universities are facing when they seek to add things like preferred name or pronoun fields in student databases. However, time and resources are well spent on these changes, and examples are popping up all over North America to show that this is both possible and necessary.

PART THREE.

WHAT TO DO

Now that you've learned about how gender works and the role of language in both gender and gender-friendliness, in Part 3 I focus on what you can do to begin building a more gender-friendly world around you.

Let me be clear: A gender-friendly world isn't a world without gender. It's not a palette of grays and beiges, or a sea of shapeless bodies in tunics and bowl cuts. It's neither a utopia nor a dystopia. A gender-friendly world is a world of gender abundance and gender joy, whether one's joy resounds in masculinity, femininity, both, or neither. Gender-friendly practices are tools for bringing this world into being, starting with where you are. Gender-friendly practices by definition do not call others into question when their appearance, behavior, needs, or feelings go against our visceral expectations for whatever category we lumped them into on sight.

In this part we'll revisit your gender-friendly road map and talk about specific actions you can implement to support people you care about who are on the transgender spectrum, or who do gender in ways unlike other people around you. I'll then show how you can practice self-care and build a community around you of people who are also committed to creating a gender-friendly world.

7.

How to Stop Telling People Who They Are, Gender-Wise, by Accident

You're the Authority on Your [XYZ], Not Me!

Gender-Friendly Ways to Talk About Partners

Gender-Friendly Ways to Talk About Babies and Kids

It's Not My Business Which Bathroom You Use!

Boring but Important: Gender-Friendly Forms

This chapter will explore the tendency to call other people into question in everyday conversations, often without meaning to or without being aware that we are doing this. I'll help you begin to recognize and avoid this habit, which I call "telling people who they are or should be" in the gender department.

Whether in person or in quick-fire text or DM exchanges, when we're chatting with others, we often tell them who they are or even who they should be with the questions we ask or by directing them to some gendered spaces but not others. This is another way we participate in gender by calling people into question, but often without asking explicit questions. And this most often happens unconsciously, without any intention on our part.

Transgender and cisgender people alike who experience this all the time know how exhausting it can be and how it can lead to self-censorship or isolation. The accumulated impact can even stop you from accessing things you need to be well, like sites of service provision (doctor, mental health services) or a gym or other recreational space, because accessing them just takes too much emotional work.

In this chapter, then, I share tips for gender-friendly language beyond using particular words. Each section describes a common situation you're likely to run into at one time or another, then explains gender-friendly ways to handle it. Sometimes we don't mean to say what we say or do what we do, but our gender-language robot selves take over. These tips are ways to stop this from happening to you. Each tip also includes extensions that adapt its basic premise to other situations.

You're the Authority on Your [XYZ], Not Me!

In Chapter 1, I shared my sister Megan's story of her experiences with infertility. In her thirties, as a woman without children, she began standing out and getting called into question by people she knew and perfect strangers alike, including while she and her husband were trying to get pregnant. Megan's story shows how question-calling can take the form of *actual questions* from well-meaning people: "Do you want kids?" or even "Why don't you have kids yet?" But question-calling can also happen nonverbally via how we react to someone with our body language, affect, and tone. Our nonverbal reactions often tell another person what they should do, like, or want, instead of holding open the possibility that there might be more to know.

I began thinking about this in my first year as a McGill undergrad when I met my friend Brianna O'Connor Hersey. Brianna had a painful autoimmune disorder where the bowel develops lesions that don't heal well or at all. When we met, Brianna was about to have surgery after many years of living with the painful effects of this condition. This involved having a portion of her bowel removed and the remaining end attached to an opening in her torso. After the surgery Brianna's body would excrete waste into disposable bags that she attached to the stoma, or opening. For most people this sounds unpleasant at best. If you haven't experienced acute illness or chronic pain, you might struggle to imagine this ever being a good option, and your reactions to hearing about it likely would be limited to concern or even pity for the person about to go through it. This was me at the time. But Brianna sat me and a few others down on the carpet in what was then the McGill Women's Union. Marker in hand, and with an abundance of fascination and enthusiasm, she drew us a diagram of her upcoming surgery and explained how the stoma would work. Brianna's affect was contagious. I, too, became excited about her surgery and its outcome. She taught us to reflect back to her the meaning of this life event for her: not unpleasant, not gross, but promising and exciting.

Brianna taught me a lesson that day about noticing my own reactions and catching myself, as well as learning to mirror others when the topic is their life, not mine. We can easily adapt this lesson for our gender-friendly tool kit. When I talked about asking someone for their pronouns, I stressed that it's important to receive the answer as if whatever that person says is exactly what you expected to hear. There's no point in respectfully asking someone for their pronouns if your reaction says their pronouns are ridiculous. There are many reasons why a person's pronouns might surprise you, but if you react instead by mirroring their affect with your tone, facial expression, and body language, you sideline what you think you "know" and instead position that person as the expert on whether something is right or wrong for them. In my experience, this is far more powerful than just telling them they know what's best.

In sum, as a gender-friendly practice, do your best to react lightly and neutrally about X until you have more information about what X means to the person at the center of it all. Try not to react in an exaggerated way that tells them how *you* believe they should think or feel. Here are some extensions of this tip:

- Try to bracket your surprise when a person first comes out to you about their gender identity (or sexual orientation). If you react with surprise, you're once again telling them who you think you are, or that it couldn't possibly be true that they are who they say they are. It's okay to have challenging or unexpected feelings about someone else's life path, but the message here is that you can have these feelings, take them away with you to process on your own or with help, *and* respond in a gender-friendly way in the moment by paying attention to your own reaction and mirroring the other as best as you can. That said, if someone you know or care about has come out to you in the past and you reacted in a negative or closed way, you might read this tip with some difficult feelings. Only you know the condition of your relationship today, but now that you know a bit more, it might be a good idea to share with them how you wish you had reacted at the time: with as much gender-friendliness as you could muster. I'll say more about this in Chapter 9.

- Women whose bodies don't align with stereotypical size expectations are constantly called into question. We usually react to a woman's dramatic weight loss by saying "You look great!" or similar. But let's say you run into a friend who has lost a significant amount of weight since the last time you saw her. What if your friend's weight loss isn't something she's into? What if it's the result of a serious illness or a stressful life event? Because the body size rules of the woman category are so rigid, we aren't used to taking these possibilities into account before speaking. Rather, we plow forward as if weight loss is always an unquestionable good, full stop. Your well-meaning compliment tells her *how she should feel* about her weight loss, and even that she didn't look great *before*. A better strategy, then, is to convey that you don't know what her body change means—that you aren't the authority on *who* she is—but that you're interested in *how* she is. The more gender-friendly practice is bracketing your surprise about her weight loss and just saying, "I haven't seen you in so long! How have you been?"

- We know that children's play and, particularly, their attempts to engage adults in various types of play, are strategies for testing rules and boundaries, including about gender. When a child invites you into their play and the play is markedly gendered—whether or not it conforms to gendered expectations—bring as much gusto as you can muster and try to stay aware of your energy levels. Do your best to remain on an even keel, and explicitly say when it's time for you to move along instead of just showing passive disinterest, which can be read as disapproval or discomfort. And if a child has a play idea that goes against the rules for their gender, try to react with no more or less enthusiasm than you would show if they asked for their favorite toy. This way, you aren't accidentally telling them whether this is an appropriate or inappropriate choice for them. Lastly, do your best not to comment on or editorialize on a child's gender-nonconforming play (etc.) within their earshot. They might not be aware that the activity is considered gender nonconforming at all, and that's both beautiful and worth preserving.

- The previous tip was about children's play, but adults play too! We each have shows or movies we like, social media accounts we follow, and hobbies or pastimes we enjoy. There are many men who would rather pick flowers or forage for mushrooms than go fishing or hunting, and just as many women who would rather the opposite. Although adults tend to be more relaxed about other adults' "play," the question-calling continues, and you can cease participating in it.

Gender-Friendly Ways to Talk About Partners

Let me just say that I'm not someone who turns down gossip. I'm as interested as anyone else in talking about who's dating who in my communities, and in queer and trans communities this means doing a lot of gender-free communication about people I don't know very well (or at all). Mercifully, there are terms for this purpose, some of which I included in the table of gender-neutral relationship terms in Chapter 6.

The past few decades have seen the rise of "partner language," or when people use the gender-neutral term *partner* to refer to a person they're in a relationship with. This wasn't always the case. I vividly remember hearing someone say "my partner" in the intimate sense for the very first time. At six years old, I was flabbergasted. I'm sure my mouth hung open as I gaped at the woman who said it and the man she had called her "partner." I knew they were together, but their connection was now unfathomable. Today saying "my partner" around a kid likely wouldn't register at all because partner language is used by all kinds of people, often because it's less diminutive than *boyfriend* or *girlfriend*. In fact, I'd even go so far as to say that, outside of contexts like business or law where *partner* has a specific connotation, calling someone "my partner" is probably always interpreted as a sign of an intimate relationship today. Like using singular *they* as a gender-neutral pronoun for a nonbinary person you know, the rise of partner language is just one more example of language changing as society changes.

While many people choose gender-neutral terms like *partner* when talking about their *own* relationships, a gender-friendly practice is using gender-neutral language when you ask or speak about *others'* relationships. For example, let's say your acquaintance mentions they're going on a date or seeing someone but doesn't offer any other information. A classic experience of many nonheterosexual men is people automatically using *she/her* pronouns to refer to that someone, and vice versa for nonheterosexual women. This is frustrating because it presumes that anyone they'd be dating is necessarily of the "opposite sex," or that the person is necessarily straight. In these instances it's more gender friendly to use singular *they* and gender-neutral terms for others' unspecified partners or dates. This doesn't tell them who you think they are, which in this case means who you think they should desire or date. Using gender-neutral language also holds open the possibility that their partner or date is a nonbinary person. As you know by now, this might just be the case! So, here's the tip, condensed: When asking or talking about another person's special someone, use gender-neutral language until you have more information. This means using *partner*, *date*, "person you're seeing," *they/them*, etc. You'll learn soon enough, by listening and mirroring a person's own language use, which terms are warranted. Here is an extension of this tip:

- **Parents,** you send valuable and generous messages to your kids about their own life possibilities when you use gender-neutral language for other people's partners, pause and ask which pronouns are appropriate in a conversation, or mirror whatever gendered language is used without necessarily asking: "Wait a minute—is that person a he or a she?" Sometimes talking about other people can be a trial balloon that your kid floats in a conversation with you when they are wondering how you'd react to news that hits closer to home: about their own relationship with gender or sexuality. You can also send your kids gender-friendly messages by intentionally using gender-neutral language to ask about their friends and their friends' friends, whether platonic or romantic. If your kids hear these messages in your home, they're more likely to share with you how they are feeling and what they are wondering about as they get older. This is perhaps the most important relationship in which to send a message that "gender is not the only thing I care about." After all, researchers have repeatedly found that supportive parent and family relationships are key protective factors for gender- and sexual-minority youth. And, even if your kids are straight, cisgender, and gender conforming, wouldn't it be wonderful if they could be sure their queer and trans friends will be welcome and safe in your home?

Gender-Friendly Ways to Talk About Babies and Kids

When you meet someone with a baby and they haven't styled the baby in a way that makes the gender extremely obvious, try using gender-neutral language. This conveys that you're interested in more

than just gender and also helps create a climate where babies don't
have to be gender styled. In such a climate parents can dress their
babies in leggings and T-shirts all the time and not have to deal with
long hair or make hairdos happen (if they don't enjoy doing so) just
to avoid a chorus of gender questions. Soon-to-be parents and new
parents can also get to feel like people are invested in their baby
beyond the gender box, and in how they themselves are doing too.
You've also learned that some babies aren't as easily assigned into one
or the other gender box, including but not only because they're intersex (see the sidebar in Chapter 1). If there were less of an imperative
to gender babies, it could mean less anxiety for many parents whose
answer to "girl or boy?" immediately calls them into question, for
any number of reasons.

There are many things worth knowing when you hear that someone you know just had a baby, but in the heat of the moment it's
easy to default to the boy-or-girl question like a robot. Here are some
other questions you can have on hand that are just as (if not more)
important. Of course, each is more or less applicable depending on
your circumstances.

- Is everyone doing okay?
- How did the delivery go?
- Was it a hospital birth?
- Do they have any family visiting?
- Do they have everything they need?
- Are they having a celebration of some kind?
- Have they had a baby before? (Here, singular *they* doesn't
  presume the gender of the birthing parent and also doesn't
  presume the number of parents.)

You can also use gender-neutral language when talking about a
kid whose gender isn't obvious, even if you think you "know." There
are many reasons to do this. Some kids, even young ones, identify
under the nonbinary umbrella. Some parents are raising their kids in

a gender-open way, using singular *they* until their kid makes their own pronoun known. And there are many children who are cisgender but gender nonconforming and whose parents dread the question-calling that arises whenever they share basic information about their lives. For example, imagine you're sitting down to a meeting with a mix of old and new faces. With a few minutes left before it starts, you turn to the person next to you and ask if she did anything fun on the weekend. "My kid had a dance competition on Saturday, so it was a bit of a gong show," she replies. This is your moment to shine, so take out your gender-friendly tool kit and consider what you might say next:

- "What kind of dance does *she* do?"
- "Did *your kid* have fun?"
- "Did *they* have fun?"

Be honest—something like number one would likely slip out, perhaps before you read this book. It might also happen again because gender-friendliness takes time to develop. If this person's dancing kid is a boy, I can feel her energy plummet and muscles tighten as she prepares to correct you: "Actually, it's my son who dances. He does tap and ballet." Because boys who dance can stand out, this person is likely bracing herself for a response that tells her, once again, how unusual her son is. As she contemplates his future, all of these messages can add up and stress her out about how he will be treated as he gets older and moves into the world without her. It can be very hard for a parent under such stress not to let it spill over and become something a kid can pick up on.

We can choose gender-friendliness instead by saying number two or three, which will probably come as a wonderful surprise. In saying "your kid" or "they," you are letting the person know that you're cool with her son being a competitive dancer or—even better, perhaps—it's as normal to you as the day is long. And for the rare parent of a nonbinary dancer whose pronouns are actually *they/them*, this tiny, insignificant nugget of gender-friendly small talk is solid gold:

to be treasured and remembered during all the gender-unfriendly moments they experience with not-you.

And so, for all of these reasons, using gender-neutral terms and singular *they*—until you have more information, not forever—is a solid gender-friendly practice in relation to kids and the loving adults in their lives.

It's Not My Business Which Bathroom You Use!

Strangers commonly ask each other for the location of the nearest bathroom. This can happen when you're both new to a space, or it can happen because you're the person working the front desk who's supposed to know these things. How we habitually respond to someone—by directing them to either "the men's" or "the women's"—tells them who we think they are and thus where we think they should go. We also send a gender-unfriendly message when we plunge into awkwardness, desperately wracking our brain for the location of the gender-neutral washroom they just asked about (and which we should find out, for just such an occasion, in advance). A gender-friendly practice is directing every asker to the gendered bathrooms (usually side by side) and the nearest gender-neutral bathroom. Here's a gender-*un*friendly example, where someone answers another person's bathroom question by inadvertently telling that person who they are:

> "Excuse me! Do you know where the bathroom is?"
> "Yes! The ladies' room is down the hall."

And here's a gender-friendly counterexample:

> "Excuse me! Do you know where the bathroom is?"
> "Yes! The gendered bathrooms are down the hall to the right, and
> there's an accessible gender-neutral bathroom just over there."

There are several reasons why sharing all the options, every time, is gender friendly. Many dads are presumed to not need a washroom with a baby changing table. Even if we feel absolutely certain which washroom the dudeliest dude in front of us requires, include all options because you never know. The gender-neutral washroom is usually also the accessible one, and by including the gender-neutral washroom in your answer you're not telling a person who they are in the ability department either.

Here are some extensions of this tip:

- Do a similar thing when someone asks you where the changing room is, whether in a store, at the gym, or anywhere else.
- Whenever an event is advertised (e.g., in a newsletter or on a website) or announced, and it will be held in a location unfamiliar to the people who might be attending, include information on bathrooms. Particularly, tell prospective attendees whether there is a gender-neutral bathroom and whether there are any accessible bathrooms. A good practice is to also share general accessibility information about the space. This way, you aren't telling people who can come to the event at all, without meaning to.
- In *any* gendered space, respond to a query with all gendered options. If you work or just happen to be in a department store and someone asks you where the shoe department is, let them know where they can find men's, women's, and kids' shoes. If you don't know, you can always point them to the store directory. After all, you can't know what they're after, and you're opening up the possibility that each of these destinations is both possible and okay.

More on Making Bathrooms Gender Friendly

It's no accident that I began this book with a bathroom story. Public bathrooms can be the hottest hot spots of gender-unfriendliness, whether or not your context has legislation that prohibits or ensures trans people's access to facilities that align with our gender identities. At the time of writing, nine US states have banned trans kids from using the bathroom at school. Florida and North Dakota have also banned trans people from using the bathroom in government-owned buildings, which can include airports, public parks, and public college or university campuses. I say that these bills ban trans people from using bathrooms altogether because the bathroom matching one's birth-assigned sex can be a place of considerable danger for some trans people.

By now there is copious research on transgender people's experiences of public bathrooms, revealing what many of us already know well: patterns of verbal harassment and physical attack. By contrast, the tired myth that transgender women pose a danger to (cisgender) women and girls in bathrooms has been repeatedly discounted, including by CNN in March 2017, when reporters contacted twenty law enforcement agencies in states with gender identity antidiscrimination legislation and found no reported instances of assault by transgender people after the legislation took effect. By contrast, in a survey of ninety-three transgender and gender-nonconforming people in Washington, DC, law scholar Jody L. Herman found that 70 percent of respondents reported denial of access, verbal harassment, and/or physical assault in gendered washrooms. If you see or hear this kind of pushback, you can reply with confidence that it's transgender people who are actually at risk in bathrooms and not the other way around. As more and more research comes out about trans children and youth's experiences, we are also learning more about the impact of gender-unfriendly school policies. A 2019 Harvard T.H. Chan School of Public Health study found that one-third of US transgender and/or nonbinary teens disallowed from using the correct bathroom (i.e., the one matching their gender identity) reported having been sexually assaulted; this stark association between bathroom access and sexual violence reveals the situation's seriousness.

Not using the bathroom also causes problems beyond experiencing harassment and violence. In the just-mentioned Washington,

DC, study, "Fifty-four percent of respondents reported having some sort of physical problem from trying to avoid using public bathrooms, all of whom reported that they 'held it.'" These problems included dehydration, urinary tract infections, and kidney infections. The same study found that most respondents have avoided going out in public because they couldn't be sure they would be able to access a safe bathroom when they needed one. When trans people are banned from using the bathroom that aligns with our gender identity, we are banned from public life. I'm sorry to say that this is increasingly the stated intention behind this kind of legislation in the US.

In Chapter 1, I talked about how gendered bathrooms, especially in states with anti-transgender bathroom bills, can also pose barriers for anyone whose gender gets called into question by others. For all of these reasons, I will share some ways to make public bathrooms into more gender-friendly spaces via signage and etiquette, and ways to make key-access bathrooms more accessible for everyone.

Signage

Signage has been the focus of a lot of trans people's bathroom advocacy in Canada and in US states with gender identity and/or gender expression antidiscrimination laws. An increasingly common practice is changing the signs on single-user accessible restrooms to make it clear that they're all-gender spaces. In my view, the best sign does away with gender altogether and actually depicts what's inside: not one man or one woman, but a toilet, accessibility features, and/or a changing table.

Another signage practice is including educational signs outside of the "men's" and "women's" bathrooms. These signs can give clear directions to the nearest gender-neutral restrooms. They can also make it crystal clear that no one may police anyone else's use of these bathrooms, which can be legally accurate in places like Canada where gender identity and gender expression discrimination are prohibited. This message could be something like "A person in here is the best judge of whether they are in the right place." Another kind of sign sometimes placed outside of ordinary gendered washrooms conveys a simple message that all are welcome: "This women's washroom is trans-inclusive," "Women's washroom—trans people welcome," etc.

Etiquette

Even in places where there are legal protections against discrimination on the grounds of gender identity and gender expression, trans people still experience hostility and violence in public restrooms. For these reasons, it's a gender-friendly practice to convey the belief that every other person in the bathroom with you is in the right place. This is another example of not telling someone who they are, as I discussed earlier in this chapter. You can convey this belief with your body language and facial expression in three ways.

1. First, you can avoid telling people they *shouldn't* be there by doing your best to not express surprise at their presence, whether verbally or nonverbally. For example, on the rare occasions where I have no choice but to use a gendered bathroom (I usually choose the women's because I've been to the other side on many occasions and it often smells worse), I sometimes hear this: "Oh phew! You're a woman." Well, no, actually. So, try not to express surprise (or relief), and avoid taking secret second looks in my direction, because they aren't all that secret!

2. Second, you can convey the message that everyone is in the right place by completely ignoring the people around you, even if you feel hyperaware of someone's presence. This is a useful strategy if you are shy or an introvert.

3. My third and final—and more extrovert-friendly—suggestion is making eye contact and smiling at other people, as this indicates that they're in the right place and welcome there.

Key Access

In addition to changing familiar routines and rituals, changing familiar *structures* is also warranted if a structure itself is a hot spot.

For example, some buildings contain several office or business suites that share washrooms. These are often accessible only to clients using a key. To use a washroom in these cases you have to take a key off a hook in a very public space or ask for it in front of others. To make them harder to walk away with, the keys are often attached to large, conspicuous objects. I've seen everything from plain wooden spoons, to wooden spoons painted neon pink and neon blue, to Barbie and Ken dolls, and everything in between. This can go very badly for some people, either because they have to select a binary-gendered object in front of a bored waiting room or because they have to ask for the key to a gendered washroom in front of a bored coffee lineup.

If you work or spend time in a place like this, and you feel comfortable doing so, consider asking someone in charge what would happen if a person needed a gender-neutral washroom to plant the seed that this is a problem. This can include connecting your question to local human rights laws, if applicable. You might suggest removing Barbie and Ken in favor of two plain objects, like wooden spoons. Even if one spoon says "women" and one spoon says "men" in small writing, it's not as easy for others to see a person's selection in the waiting room and call them into question.

Boring but Important: Gender-Friendly Forms

If you recently started a job with a large company or enrolled your kid in karate, you probably realize by the end of Chapter 7 that forms are typically gender unfriendly. They don't typically specify legal or preferred first name, or ask for pronouns. Gender is often asked, even if completely irrelevant, like when joining a consumer rewards program or signing up for a class that isn't gender specific. There's usually a "gender box"—two deceptively simple options labeled "male" and "female." This is actually a "sex box," and it's unclear to many transgender people how they should answer this question, with nonbinary people left out altogether.

If you are the boss where you work or spend time, you have the power to make your organization's forms gender friendly. Here are some tips (if you aren't the boss, consider bringing these up the chain):

- Figure out whether you actually need people's gender information. If you don't, get rid of the gender question. Some sectors have legal reporting requirements to ensure that girls and women are equally accessing a service or program. Even so, you can still ditch the boxes in favor of a write-in gender question or keep boxes but have actual gender (not sex) options: man or boy, woman or girl, nonbinary or similar, and prefer not to say. Don't put transgender men and transgender women in a position of having to tick a separate box from their cisgender counterparts.
- Add an optional pronoun field.
- Make sure you actually need to collect a person's legal first name(s), and if you don't, explicitly collect preferred first name(s) only.

Sometimes a gender-unfriendly form comes from a third party, like an insurance or benefits company. We might be the person walking a new hire through the form. Even in these situations, we have a gender-friendly way forward: letting everyone (not only some people who stand out) know that the current form doesn't work for everyone, and that if they have other information to share, they are welcome to tell us or to write in any blank space. You can also point to the "gender (sex) box" and just say "which one would you like me to check?" instead of "male or female"? These are very different ways of asking the question, one infinitely more gender friendly than the other.

8.

An Action Plan for Standing Up Beside Your Person

---

1. Pay Attention

2. Opt Out of Question-Calling

3. Identify Hot Spots

4. Take Action

5. Make a Power Move

Now You Have Your Gender-Friendly Tool Kit

In Chapter 2 you began sketching your gender-friendly road map, noticing and making observations about the people around you, including how they do or don't fit into how gender works in the spaces you share, whether personal, work-related, or social. Now we return to your gender-friendly road map and explore what it looks like to follow that map by taking practical steps to open up gender in the space you have mapped out.

You might be particularly invested in taking action because you're a family member, parent, friend, or partner of a trans person. How great would it be if your person could enjoy a visit with your extended family, or even just come with you to spin class? Or you might not have a particular trans and/or gender-nonconforming person in mind right now. In this case, by following your road map you're acting on your awareness that, sooner or later, someone will enter the space who is transgender (which, as we've seen, could mean many things) or whose way of doing gender transgresses the gender rules that you now know are enforced where you are.

The practical steps I offer in this chapter are:

1. Pay attention
2. Opt out of question-calling
3. Identify hot spots
4. Take action
5. Make a power move

1. Pay Attention

First, pay attention to the question-calling when it happens (you can go back to the table in Chapter 2 for examples of what this can look like). Ask yourself:

- If there's laughter, is it the laughing-with or laughing-at variety, and is the "laughing with" actually what it claims to be?
- If there's gossip, who gossips with whom? Is there any effort at subtlety, or is it open season?
- If there's sarcasm and eye-rolling, is it just one person or does everyone participate?
- Are the previous examples whole-office or whole-family (etc.) activities, or do some people opt out? *Can* people opt out, or do they themselves get called into question when they try?
- Is there anyone who does or could do X and not be called into question? Is this you?

You'll learn a lot about how gender works in that space or community of people once you begin paying attention, and you'll probably want to make some adjustments to your road map. This is to be expected.

2. Opt Out of Question-Calling

Second, try to recognize when *you* participate in question-calling, and do your best to opt out, whether this means stopping all at once or by degrees. Opting out doesn't only mean stopping the laughter from happening altogether. You might not have that power (which might sound weird, but remember that this book is for people of all ages and who are facing many different situations). Opting out can mean:

- Not laughing yourself, or not laughing in a way that amplifies or encourages the laughter.
- Keeping a neutral facial expression and not making eye contact with others who are participating in the question-calling.
- Making eye contact with the standing-out person and sending nonverbal messages of support. This can be a smile, a tilt of the head, or even a hand on the heart.
- Verbally checking in.
- Walking over to the standing-out person and starting another conversation.
- Lifting up the person by drawing on or bringing up something they're proud of.

Another thing you can do is share your concerns with people who have the power to help. This is why, in Chapter 2 and in this section, I asked you to think about who in that space could "get away with" standing out and who could make the question-calling stop, because they might have power that you don't have. This doesn't just mean the power to make formal rules, like a parent or a boss. It could also be the power to stop the laughing because when that person stops, everybody stops. And sometimes we can't opt out entirely because we risk becoming a target too. This is a bad situation, but it's important to be real about whether you're at risk yourself and how you can stay okay.

3. Identify Hot Spots

Third, keep an eye out for hot spots: times or places where the question-calling is either enabled or inevitable. Often hot spots happen in or around activities where people are divided into girls and boys, or women and men, or where people are invited to make assumptions about others on the basis of limited information. But a hot spot can also be a person (or more than one) who continually creates a gender-unfriendly or downright unsafe place for gender nonconformity of any kind, whether in general or for a particular person who stands out. Think about what might neutralize hot spots in your space or change how they play out.

If you find yourself in a hot spot, there are some things you can do right away that don't involve educating others about gender and how it's doing harm in this moment, whether based on your own expertise or on what I've shared with you here. This is how people can get hung up and do nothing: by thinking that the only thing they can do is forcefully intervene and risk getting into a sparring match about something that they might not feel they know enough about (at least not yet). An educational intervention is an option, but *it is not the only one.* Here are two other things you can do to lessen a hot spot's impact in the moment if you don't feel like you can intervene explicitly and directly:

- Invite the standing-out person to do something else with you instead of remaining within or near the hot spot. This could look like asking them to help you with something, which would make you the reason why they're leaving.
- Change the group caught up in the hot spot, either by adding or subtracting people. When someone leaves or someone new enters an interaction, dynamics shift, new conversation topics emerge, and breaks in conversation allow for change.

4. Take Action

By taking action I mean doing concrete things to anticipate hot spots and doing your best to cool them down before someone who stands out is harmed by them. Often, this harm looks like misgendering, and can include the use of incorrect pronouns, names, terms, and rigidly gendered language more broadly, or it can look like being grouped along with others into the wrong gender box (verbally or actually). But the harm can also look like different kinds of violence. In taking action, you are trying your best to avoid the likelihood, frequency, and severity of all of these things.

To illustrate taking action, I'll place you in a scenario where you're supporting someone who stands out in the gender department and is being called into question in some way, or who will *foreseeably* stand out in a space or group of people you have in common. This could be a child, sibling, coworker, partner, or friend. Your goal is to take action in order to make this a more gender-friendly place for your person while also not burning it all down and salting the earth. In other words, this approach assumes that this is a space or group that offers some good or helpful things that you need or benefit from and that stands to do the same for your person. First, though, some changes are required.

Imagine that you've already drawn your road map by reflecting on the gender boundaries here and how various people tend to participate in question-calling when these boundaries are crossed. You've begun to follow your road map by:

- Paying attention
- Recognizing and beginning to opt out of the question-calling yourself
- Identifying hot spots among the usual structures or routines that happen there

Each section that follows contains an action step, and I pull out takeaways from each step for particular situations (especially those that feature parent-child relationships).

Help Your Person Get Ready

Have a conversation together about where they're at and how they're doing these days, especially if you haven't in a while. Ask open questions about how much work they've had to do lately to have their needs met (e.g., correcting, explaining), and how much energy they're bringing into the space, event, group, or gathering and their interactions with the people you both know will be in it. Help them think through the kinds of conversations they're able and willing to have, which ones you can front-load beforehand and with whom (more on this to come), and the conversations that need to stay off-limits. For example, are they currently able to answer questions about their gender or have intellectual conversations about whether their pronoun is grammatically correct?

Once they've identified some sore topics and boundaries with your help, affirm that they have every right to draw the lines that they need to draw. Talk about constructive ways to draw those lines if these topics arise. Brainstorm a few ways they can leave unwelcome interactions, and be prepared to help them leave if necessary. A useful tip to share with them (even if they might end up using it on you, too, someday) is to pretend their phone vibrated, pick it up, and pretend there's someone there. This is an example of making a boundary without explicitly asserting a boundary, and can be a useful tool, especially for a person who may not feel comfortable openly advocating for their boundaries with a more powerful personality.

- A broader takeaway from this action step is the importance of standing beside, and not in front of, someone else. If you're close to a person who is standing out gender-wise, checking in and working *with* them is better than going rogue and doing it all by yourself. However, you may not feel comfortable doing so depending on your relationship. This doesn't mean you can't take action, just that the action you take should not be speaking *for* them. For example, a takeaway from this book is that everyone, including you, has skin in the gender game. Another takeaway is that transgender people are either present or will be present in the spaces where you spend time. Your own comfort or the space's capacity to welcome gender diversity—not X person's needs—are good reasons to act.

Recruit Someone Else to Help You Out

From drawing your road map you've already got a mental list of the people who will be present in the space you are thinking about. Use your gut and gender expertise to feel out whether one of them could be called in to take on the work of (gently and kindly) reminding people when they slip up, answering some of the most common questions, or supporting you when you try to tweak a tradition or ritual. Even if you're in a support role, the work of correcting can become exhausting, and ensuring that at least one other person is on board to help out can mean you will have more energy for self-care and supporting your person. You may want to talk with your person about who this someone can be, unless their gender identity and pronouns are already common knowledge. Who knows! Your person may want to be there when you have the conversation, and their presence might work wonders if they feel safe and supported.

This action step is a reminder to look to others around you as resources and not obstacles, as best as you can. Just because they passively participate in question-calling doesn't mean that they know they're doing it or that they're bad people. They also might not have felt like they have a choice, lest they become targets themselves.

Tweak Familiar Rituals or Routines

This action step is about deprioritizing "what we do here" or "what has always been done" and instead prioritizing what is needed in order to make a space more gender friendly. If there's an entrenched ritual or routine in your space that you have recognized as a hot spot, it doesn't need to keep on going in its current form. It's okay to prioritize everyone's well-being and participation in that space over things that people have come to expect and rely on when they're already comfortable there. And don't fear awkwardness or the discomfort of change. Any amount of awkwardness is better than letting business as usual be a source of harm.

Activities and Events

Gender boxes tend to come into the foreground when strangers or people who don't know each other well (whether at all or because changes have taken place, gender-related or not) have to interact. There isn't much to rely on when you don't know someone, and something we're often presumed to have in common is a particular relationship to the two gender boxes. Well, you know by now that this isn't a good bet for many reasons.

It's helpful to structure ice-breaker activities and get-to-know-you events so that people's participation doesn't just fall back on gender expectations out of necessity. If there's going to be a "people bingo" activity (i.e., where strangers have to find other strangers who have a particular interest, experience, or characteristic), offer to review the bingo sheet and keep an eye out for questions that assume membership in just one gender box. Questions like these will authorize participants to read and infer gender in ways that aren't gender friendly.

You can also help nudge others away from explicitly or implicitly gender-divided activities, including by stepping into a leadership role yourself, if you can. This might be for an office party or a friend's prewedding event, for example.

Lastly, events beyond an hour in length mean that people have to use a bathroom in order to participate. If someone needs a gender-neutral bathroom, asking its whereabouts can produce a gender hot spot for the asker, making them stand out to anyone who overhears or receives gossip about the ask. The emcee or host can include the location of all bathrooms in their welcoming remarks. If there is no gender-neutral bathroom, and one cannot be designated gender-neutral during the event, you might say something like "We regret that there is no gender-neutral bathroom nearby. However, [share the nearest one, like a staff single-stall washroom behind the scenes that guests can ask to use if needed, or across the road at McDonald's]."

Gift-Giving Situations

Many holiday rituals involve gift giving, which easily shifts into gender-unfriendly territory when people don't know each other very well or when someone wants to send a message about what they think the recipient *should* want. Gift giving can be awkward at best among mere acquaintances, but imagine if a standing-out person has to open gifts that are very clearly not intended for someone of their gender identity or gender expression *and* take care of the gift giver's feelings. Think dolls given every year to a gender-nonconforming girl by a grandmother who wants to encourage traditionally feminine interests. I also think here of the annual office Secret Santa, where women get smelly soaps and men get golf tees, or the "teenage girl" and "teenage boy" gift sets that you can buy in any chain drugstore, with pink or blue products as well as *BOY* or *GIRL* in huge letters on the package. It isn't always this dramatic, but gift giving among people who don't know each other well can most certainly be a gender hot spot.

There are things you can do to dial down the impact. First, and most obviously, you can try to stop the gift giving from happening altogether, but that's not likely to go over very well with others. Another strategy is to suggest that individual gift giving not happen this year, but that your group, office, or family make a collective donation to a nonprofit or other organization that echoes values that you all share, and take time to celebrate the accomplishment of raising and making your donation. If that fails, you can discourage public gift opening in order to make the occasion less exposing for someone likely to be misgendered by their gifts. One more tip for a Secret Santa or gift-drawing scenario: Take over the name drawing, and stack the deck so that you or another supportive person gives a gift to the person who stands out or is likely to stand out.

- **Parents** have a few more options, given that you're placed in a more protective and authoritative role vis-à-vis your child. You could share information about your kid's interests that explicitly discourages "girl" or "boy" gifts but doesn't out their gender identity (if that is a concern). Gift cards for movies, a major online retailer, or a local (non-gender-specific) business are good choices here. If your kid is a teenager, this year you could suggest that children in the family receive gifts, but that teens and adults together make donations on the family's behalf, as I suggested before. And if you can't discourage public gift opening among your family, you could ask your kid if they want to skip the extended-family present opening (if necessary, you can offer the rest of the group a reason for their absence that makes sense in context) and have a more private one later on.

- Times when a standing-out person is going to receive recognition of some kind (birthday, award ceremony, wedding, baby shower, etc.) are likely to be gender hot spots, so be prepared during these occasions to help nudge recognition away from unwanted or inappropriate gendering as best as you can, and as needed. Particularly if the honoree has *they/them* or other gender-neutral pronouns, encourage the person making the formal remarks to write them down, practice, and not go off script.

Build One-on-One Time for Less Misgendering

For transgender people who have changed pronouns, most misgendering that we see happens when people around us have to talk about us. In a one-on-one conversation a person has to go far out of their way to use a third-person pronoun (*they, she, he*). We just ask questions and answer them without talking about each other. And so, a gender-friendly action step is to encourage one-on-one formats because misgendering can be more likely in group gatherings.

Furthermore, while question-calling happens in one-on-one conversations and even among mere acquaintances, as we've seen, it's also less exposing than the kind that can happen in larger groups. And so, an easy way to reduce the risk of misgendering and other kinds of question-calling is to pare down group size or select one-on-one formats.

- Think about changing the format or duration of a familiar ritual or routine to lessen its impact, particularly the impact of repeated misgendering. This might mean having shorter activity-based visits in groups instead of longer conversation-heavy ones. Or it might mean having phone calls instead of visits.
- **Parents**, if there are visiting family members whom your trans kid wants to connect with but isn't ready to come out to, you can reduce the risk of misgendering by facilitating one-on-one time. You can ask your child if there's a particular activity they would like to share with that family member, and perhaps deliver the invitation yourself in an encouraging way. In addition to providing low-risk connection, one-on-one time might be an opportunity for your child to come out on their own. Of course, I suggest checking in and strategizing with them beforehand.

Set a Proactive Boundary

If you are in a position of power or authority, you can work proactively and in the background to make changes that enable everyone to be and remain well where you are. A difficult conversation with someone who actively creates gender-unfriendly hot spots or initiates harmful question-calling behaviors doesn't necessarily have to involve or take energy from the person who stands out, whether transgender or not. If a norm of your space is that it is gender friendly and welcoming to people no matter how they do gender, then this person's behavior can be addressed as a problem for the space and not just individualized to the person targeted by the behavior. Your private conversation with them might be an opportunity for the person to air their beliefs and feel heard. It's also an opportunity to call them in by lifting up their strengths and contributions to the space or group, and remind them of the community's values that they also share and benefit from. But under no circumstances should this airing, hearing, and calling-in require the participation of persons targeted and harmed by the behavior. This is the leader's responsibility alone. That said, it's always okay for the leader—be they a parent, supervisor, administrator, teacher, principal, or other person in charge—to reach elsewhere for support or resources in order to carry out this responsibility, and to consult with the targeted person or persons, if warranted.

- **Parents**, if there's a particular family member who you know is unsupportive of trans people or on the record as touting particularly rigid beliefs about gender, find some time to authentically connect with them before they share space with your kid. If they live nearby, make a point to try and see them a few times before a planned holiday or event. As you get closer to the event, plan to have a conversation. Sit down with them alone, take their hands, look them in the eyes, and tell them how much you appreciate, love, and/or care for them. Tell them how much you cherish the holiday memories you have with them and your family, and how glad you are that they are joining you.

   Then firmly but gently draw a boundary. Let them know that you fully support your kid's gender identity, gender expression, and related needs, and that you're concerned the family member doesn't understand or agree. You might even affirm that they're free to have their own beliefs. You aren't telling them what to believe, but insisting that these beliefs cannot be aired around your child. Sometimes it helps people to hear that a key determinant of a trans person's well-being is a supportive family environment (especially for kids), and that this is the basis for your decision. I suggest doing this ahead of time because your family member may have anger or resentment about this boundary. You may have to be the container for some of this, if you are able to, so it can come out in a way that does not directly harm your child but offers an opportunity for your family member to feel heard. That said, we also know from attitudinal research that people who have personal contact with a (known) transgender person are less likely to hold negative views of transgender people. For this reason, try your best to keep the door open for their questions, now and in the future. Being around your trans kid might bring more willingness and desire to learn, which you can help with. However, it's always okay to make the call that it's not worth the risk.

Share Information with Others

Before I get going in this section, know that there are few if any situations where it's okay to out a transgender adult who is not out, without their express knowledge and consent. *Do not do this*, except in exceptional circumstances (e.g., if it's somehow medically necessary to disclose this information in an actual medical emergency where they are incapacitated), or if the circumstances of your relationship somehow make it a thinkable thing to do. I can't tell you when it would be okay, but I can tell you that it almost never is, and can even put someone in danger. The default is don't.

That said, part of making a space more gender friendly could mean sharing information about someone's gender and gender-related needs, but only with their consent if this information is not public knowledge. The person might not be immediately readable as their gender identity, but will have to come out in order to have their gender identity respected and their correct name and pronouns used. Or the person might be currently changing how they do gender, whether through social transition, medical transition, both, or neither. In any case, it might be necessary to convey information that someone is on the transgender spectrum, and what that means for others. For example, I'm publicly out about being nonbinary and about my pronouns; that said, I sometimes find myself in a space where I don't know anybody and am not known. If I did know someone there, it would be useful to me if they shared in advance this publicly available information with others.

The best-case scenario is that a person communicates this themself, on their own terms, and receives a supportive response. However, you might have inferred from using your gender expertise and drawing your road map that this will place the person in harm's way. Or, and perhaps more likely, they might infer this using their own expertise gleaned from being a trans or gender-nonconforming person in a rigidly gendered world, which means learning how to stay safe as best as one can.

Let's assume that it has fallen to you, with their consent, to share information about their gender needs and/or that they are transgender. You have two paths before you, depending on how you imagine this might go using your gender expertise and your road map of how gender works where you are. The first path is taken when you expect resistance, and the second path is taken when you don't expect much or any resistance.

When You Expect Resistance

First, I refer you to the previous action step on setting boundaries, which will come in handy here too. The following are some general tips for having this conversation:

- Be clear, neutral, and matter-of-fact. Convey with your facial expression, body language, and tone of voice that this information is significant but not bad. Your gender-friendly job is to model how to best receive this information via your example.
- Ensure that the conversation is happening in private, with no possibility of anyone overhearing. This is important to allow the person to have a difficult reaction with you, where you can witness and absorb its impact, and not to bottle it up only to

let it out and negatively affect the group's dynamic or harm the person in question later on.

- Find a balance between words that you infer are familiar to the person you are speaking with and words understood by the person who you are supporting by sharing this information with others.
  - **Parents**, you may have to use terms or names that your kid isn't comfortable with in order to share this information, at least at first, so the person knows who and what you're talking about. That's okay. It's likely that your kid would, too, if they were having this conversation.
- Be ready to explain some very practical implications (i.e., say how this information changes the way they should interact with and talk about this person). Ideally, this is based on a conversation that you have had with this person about their needs (see the list of "interview" questions I provided in Chapter 6, particularly if the person is a kid).
- Remember that the purpose of doing this is to share the load otherwise borne by the trans or gender-nonconforming person in question. For this reason, it is very okay to shield them from a difficult reaction by editing out some of the key harmful details. As a self-care strategy, for example, I do not encourage people in my life to fill me in on all of the mistakes that others make with my pronouns, or to pass on all of the moments in which they've received difficult responses when I come up. I just do not need more reasons to be exhausted in a binary-obsessed world. That said, do not withhold information that pertains to safety or make any safety decisions on your person's behalf without consulting them.

Bearing these tips in mind, here is a basic script for sharing information about a person in your space with someone who will likely have a difficult reaction to this news: "You know that X is going to join us [add detail]. X is a transgender person, and this means that X uses [pronouns] and accesses gendered activities and spaces for [gender identity]." There will likely be some reaction. Next, it's important to draw a very firm line: "You likely have some questions, which is perfectly okay, and I can help you to find answers. But you need to know that I am prioritizing X's safety and well-being. X isn't going anywhere until they choose to leave for their own reasons. You need to tell me if you can't participate in a gender-friendly [space, workplace, etc.] in good faith, and do your best to use X's pronouns [etc.]. Time to adjust is okay, but it is not an option for us to make X uncomfortable or unsafe. If you have questions or need resources in order to do this, come see me."

- Here is a modification for when a mutual friend's or acquaintance's (etc.) gender identity or gender expression has recently changed, and you are sharing this information with someone likely to have a difficult reaction: "You've known X for a while now, and before you see them next time, it's important for you to know that they are transgender. There are many different ways that people can be transgender, and for X this means [...]. X has changed their (etc.) name to Y, and their (etc.) pronouns to [...]. X is also going to look different." Then proceed with the previous script, starting with "You likely have some questions..."
- **Parents,** here's a modified version for sharing this information about your kid with another member of your family: "I know that you love X very much, and before you see X next time, it's important for you to know that they are transgender. There are many different ways that people can be transgender, and for X this means [...]. X has changed their (etc.) name to Y, and their (etc.) pronouns to [...]." The rest of this conversation can be guided by what I shared in the previous action step on boundaries: calling in, allowing a space for the person to vent (while keeping yourself safe and okay), and drawing a boundary. As in the previous script, you might also ask them to let you know if this is something they can respect: "When we spend time

together, I will prioritize X's well-being, which means that you need to tell me if you can't do this. If you can't, I have to make choices that protect X, because that's my primary responsibility."

When You Don't Expect (Much) Resistance

The second path is taken when you don't expect much or any resistance from a person when you share that someone is transgender or gender nonconforming. This is likely the case because the person you're speaking with already has some knowledge of gender diversity or knows people under the transgender umbrella, whether inside or outside of your shared space. In this conversation the person isn't starting from zero or from a gender-unfriendly place, but they still might be surprised by the news if this is the first person they personally know to come out as transgender, for example.

Even when you expect little or no resistance, you can use your facial expression, body language, and tone of voice to convey that this information is no big deal. You might be fibbing a bit (it might still feel new or like a big deal to you), but in this moment you're doing the important work of modeling and reminding. Here is a basic script: "FYI, X is transgender, and has said it's okay for me to share that with you. X is going by Y now, and using [...] pronouns." Like in the first and more challenging pathway, it's important to be ready with practical implications, including whether this person can share this information with others (or not), and if so, whom.

Plan for Downtime

Having little privacy or being in large groups for long periods of time, even if they're full of well-meaning people, often means the familiar combination of advocating, correcting, and explaining, for trans or gender-nonconforming people and those walking alongside us. This can take a toll, so it's vital that there are breaks in the rhythm, whether this means quiet time, alone time, or outside time. Ensuring downtime is a gender-friendly practice because it creates an opportunity to recharge.

Whether you're planning a whole-group event, like a company retreat, wedding, or family holiday, or you're implementing routines in a long-term shared space, like an office or school classroom, make sure there's unstructured downtime. With younger groups some structure might be needed so that this time remains peaceful and restful. During this time people can reach outside of the group for the support or validation that they receive from others they *choose* to be in contact with, and this can be good for all sorts of reasons. This can look like bending family time device rules for a trans kid and letting them scroll for a little while. Trans adolescents, in particular, have flocked to the Internet to find safety, community, and affirmation, especially during and after the COVID-19 pandemic. Keeping them from their devices, whether as policy or punishment, can cause significant distress. This is also a time for people to catch up and check in with themselves in order to make sure that they're doing okay. And it helps you make sure to get some recharge time for yourself.

- **Parents and partners**, it's vital to factor in your *own* energy expenditure when you plan large group time that includes your kid, particularly with family. Go potluck, buy a pie crust, or order a pizza. The time you save is time well spent on self-care, and that means you can also be more present and supportive if needed. As plans come together I also suggest leaving a buffer zone between the last day of your family festivities and the time when your child has to go back to school.

5. Make a Power Move

In this last step, I'll describe how you can make a "power move," or how you can advocate for yourself or someone else by doing things that lawyers do when advocating on behalf of a client. I call this a "power move" because lawyers are very good at sounding and acting like they are powerful, which often means wielding the power of information (i.e., knowing better than someone else what is legal and what is against a law or a policy).

I'll give you an example, which puts you in the shoes of a **parent** or other supporting adult in a trans or gender-nonconforming kid's life. When I talked about gendered language in Chapter 6, I listed questions that can help a trans kid think through their gendered language needs. Once the kid has thought through their answers, what now? Well, it may be time to make a meeting with their school's principal or vice principal. Before the meeting, get ready to make a power move. This can look like:

- Writing up the kid's answers into a set of clear asks for different adults at school (e.g., principal, different subject teachers, and so on). The clearer the asks, the more actionable they are and the easier it will be to track whether or not they are being respected.
- Coming prepared to talk about best-fit bathroom, locker room, uniform, and intramural sports or athletics options. It's likely these topics will come up too.
- Helping the kid make detailed oral or written notes as soon as possible after a relevant experience, such as persistent misgendering or harassment.
- Coming up with good-enough, better, and best solutions to each problem the kid is experiencing.
- Anticipating the school's response to each ask or solution and planning how to respond, including where you stand your ground and where you compromise.
- Finding whether your school district has a relevant policy—a document that tells school staff what to do in situations like this one—and getting ready to say how it applies here. (If your school is in an Ontario public or Catholic school district, you can find your policies on my website, www.gegi.ca. By 2026, everyone in Canada should be able to find their school board's policies there.)

After the meeting, keep your power move going. Follow up with a crisp email that thanks the principal (etc.), lists what they agreed to do, and restates the date of your follow-up meeting—don't leave without one! Check in regularly with the kid and be the person who keeps records of, for example, when, where, and by whom they are misgendered. These records can be used later on to advocate at a higher level, such as with a superintendent or director of education, if change isn't happening at the school. Keep notes organized by date

A LOVE LETTER TO TRANS FLORIDIANS, SASKATCHEWANIANS, AND NEW BRUNSWICKERS

Unfortunately, in 2024, whether a trans student's pronouns must be respected at school depends on where you are. Two Canadian provinces (New Brunswick and Saskatchewan) now require parental consent for a student under sixteen to have their preferred name and pronouns used at school. This is such a clear human rights violation that the government of Saskatchewan had to invoke a little-used rule allowing it to legislate against the *Canadian Charter of Rights and Freedoms*. Florida passed a bill that bans staff from "calling students pronouns that differ from their biological sex." This quote is from a *Time* headline on the bill, and if you read Chapter 1, you likely see that it conflates pronouns with "biological sex" as if they are the same thing. They are not. Many human languages, such as Estonian, Finnish, and (spoken) Mandarin, do not have gendered third-person pronouns, and sex is assigned at birth across the world. This is just one of many indications that the movement against transgender rights in the US and elsewhere is not grounded in fact or science (more in Chapter 9).

To trans kids and their supporting adults in states like Florida or provinces like Saskatchewan and New Brunswick, know that you are seen, believed, and loved, and that a whole lot of people are on your side. That includes me. The heroes at LGBT YouthLine in Canada (https://youthline.ca) and the Trevor Project in the US (https://thetrevorproject.org) are also here for you.

so you can show a timeline of what has happened, including meetings you have had with the school.

While this book is most likely in an adult's hands, I want to reach out to my trans kid reader and say that these are all things you can do yourself, if you feel safe and okay doing so. If you don't have a supportive adult in your family, www.gegi.ca has ideas on how you can find one in your school or community who can help you advocate, even if you aren't in Canada. There are more tips on the site and in a document my research team created with a group of experts on gender diversity, education, and law (www.gegi.ca/wp-content/uploads/2021/05/The-Gegi-Curriculum-May-2021.pdf).

To my readers who are trans or gender-nonconforming adults, or who are working to make a space outside of your family more gender friendly, my tips for making a power move are equally for you. More and more companies, including in the US, have policies that you can bring with you into a meeting when your gender-related needs are not being respected. Connecting your situation to policy, making and keeping records, anticipating responses, and coming up with good-better-best solutions are solid ways to move forward in any challenging situation.

Now You Have Your Gender-Friendly Tool Kit

Now you have an array of gender-friendly strategies that you can put to work from today onward. You know how to take stock of your spaces, use language, take action, and make a power move, but you also understand the more subtle role of tools like your body language, facial expression, and tone of voice. You have a sense of why gender-friendly language and practice are needed, and a starting place to begin putting them to work where you are.

9.

Caring for Yourself and Growing Your Gender-Friendly Community

It's Hard Sometimes: How to Face the Challenges of Being Gender Friendly

How to Debunk False Arguments Against Gender-Friendly Change

Tips for Taking a Leadership Role with Others

Last Word

You made it! Welcome to the last chapter, where I pull the book's threads together and give you some tools to sustain your gender-friendly efforts once you get going. First, I talk about some potential challenges of speaking and acting in ways that create openness around you for all the different ways that gender is lived, whether this is inside, outside, or transcending the female/girl/woman and male/boy/man boxes. These challenges look different for different people in different places, and it's important to be real about why doing this can be hard sometimes. I offer some ways to mitigate these challenges.

The next section offers strategies for debunking erroneous arguments that have taken root against gender-neutral language use and other gender-friendly practices intended to make institutions and everyday life welcoming of how everyone lives gender, including but not limited to transgender people. It's important to be able to speak back to these arguments, to the best of your ability, so that your gender-friendly efforts aren't derailed and people around you receive accurate information. If you're cisgender, it's also important to speak back because in some US and even Canadian contexts, transgender people are learning that we can't do so ourselves anymore without serious consequences.

Because all of this is easier if you aren't going it alone, the very last section shares tips for inviting other people into the work with you. Among other things, this means trying your best to expect good things from others, even if they haven't thought a lot about these issues before, and celebrating small changes. The more you become invested in this project, and the more you begin to understand its importance, the harder it is to stay rooted in the memory of your own starting place. This is as true for trans people as it is for anyone else. Like I said in Chapter 2, gender-friendliness is a practice of humility for all of us, myself included.

It's Hard Sometimes: How to Face the Challenges of Being Gender Friendly

Being gender friendly can be hard, particularly when you're getting started. Anytime we make a change to our behavior, others take notice. Sometimes our friends, family, or colleagues can pinpoint and name the change, and at other times they just feel the change as a mounting irritation. When we opt out of question-calling, for example, and stop laughing at things we've always laughed at in the past, this simple action can be a really, really big deal for those around us. They might feel judged or looked down on, even if we didn't say a single word about why we aren't laughing anymore or about *them* having done anything wrong.

Noted feminist scholar Sara Ahmed calls this the "killjoy" phenomenon. She points out the disruptive force of just not going along anymore, or even just showing up when people start seeing you as a killjoy who doesn't go along anymore. For this reason, in Chapter 8, I offered degrees of opting out instead of a stark choice between stopping the laughter altogether and being part of the problem. Opting out by degrees isn't being a passive bystander. It's using your expertise about this time, this place, and these people to calibrate your action for impact and the safety of all concerned (including you). But even if you go carefully and thoughtfully in your gender-friendly efforts, it can be lonely sometimes. In what follows I offer suggestions for managing the isolation that can result when you find yourself going against the grain, whether for the first time or in a new way.

Take Care of Yourself Too

You might be reading this book because you want to support the transgender and/or gender-nonconforming people in your life. This is an excellent reason. A common message of this and other resources is that, generally speaking, trans people have it worse in the gender department. This is a claim that has been tested through research time and time again. However, this reality does *not* mean that a cisgender reader doesn't need support in the gender department. Yes, the trans people in your life likely face difficulty because they stand out and are called into question, to varying degrees and with varying consequences. But right now, being someone who takes action to loosen up gender can also mean standing out, getting called into question, and sometimes experiencing harm. There must be no guilt attached to naming this experience and its difficulty. Unfortunately, I often see the guilt manifest before my very eyes, and this has got to stop.

Try Not to Feel Guilty about Self-Care

I'll give an example. After I give a public lecture or a workshop, adult attendees often seek me out to chat because they have a trans kid and a question about supporting them. To these conversations I bring two goals:

1. First, I want to empower the parent to facilitate clear and practical conversations with their kid about the kid's own needs, because they know best (see my action steps in Chapter 8 for more).
2. Second—and more relevant here—I want to ask the parent how *they're* doing and project, with everything I have (facial

expression, body language, tone, and actual words—that is, my gender-friendly tool kit), my authentic belief that how they're doing matters too.

What happens next is very telling. Once we've chatted about, say, how they handle an unsupportive family member while supporting their trans kid, I pivot toward how *the parent* is doing as they balance loving their kid and not wanting to lose their family member. I get one of two reactions: like I revealed myself to be an alien being or like I returned their beloved lost dog. Both signal bafflement. This reaction often yields to an insistence that they're fine, it's the kid they're worried about, etc. Of course they're worried about their kid, first and foremost. But I'm saddened by the predictability of the baffled reaction: that it's so unlikely that I would care about and value *their* well-being too.

Consider Outside Support

I leave these conversations only when I've affirmed that the person's well-being *is* tremendously important, and that it's crucial to be real about how they're doing. As a firm believer in psychotherapy (which in my view should be free for everyone, everywhere) and a longtime client of my own therapist, I make sure to open up the possibility that mental health support can be warranted when your life circumstances unsettle the relationships you depend on for identity or sustenance, or make you alarmingly visible in ways you've never experienced before. Being real about this with yourself isn't blaming your trans (etc.) loved one or saying they're the problem. Rather, the problem is the gender-unfriendly world in which you stand in solidarity with them, and with others like them too.

Accessing professional mental health support is one way of being real with yourself about the isolation that can come with gender-friendliness, regardless of the circumstances or relationships in which you're doing this work. Even if you don't need professional support at the moment, you likely do need support of some kind. In

PARENT POWER!

Parents of transgender people didn't always visibly participate in public debates or do public advocacy work like many do now. I see trans people's parents involved in a lot of low-key advocacy too. Often the friendly cisgender person who invited me to come speak at their workplace turns out to be a trans kid's parent. They are coming to realize that they want their kid to be able to have a job someday, but their own workplace is not yet gender friendly.

Across North America there are highly active parent advocacy groups, like Gender Creative Kids in Canada and the Parents for Transgender Equality National Council (under the auspices of the Human Rights Campaign) in the US. These groups do educational and lobbying work around trans and broader gender-diversity issues. If you are a parent of a trans child or youth and they are the focus of your gender-friendly efforts, these organizations might be good places to find support outside of your immediate spaces.

Chapter 1, I drew a connection between my sister Megan's close friendships with other twin mums and my close friendships with people who just get me, gender-wise, and seamlessly meet my needs. Sometimes these friends are other trans people, and sometimes they aren't. These friendships offer Megan and me a safe harbor where what we are, do, or care about is just completely unremarkable: where it doesn't stand out. I suggest seeking out similarly safe harbors for yourself: finding other people—including *outside* of your immediate spaces—who are also working at gender-friendliness, whatever that looks like where they are. I'll come back to cultivating others *within* your spaces later on.

It's Okay to Be Honest with Your Person

This is another self-care strategy geared toward people who picked up this book because of a transgender and/or gender-nonconforming person in your life. As a nonbinary person and singular *they/them* user, I've long understood that being me requires my people to make an extra effort. My people also have particular needs that require extra effort from me, which I put in as best as I can. However, the kind of extra effort that I and my pronouns need can make my people stand out much more than they might otherwise.

In moments when you're already tired or uncomfortable, they-ing your they-person (etc.) to a mere acquaintance or a complete stranger can be a coming out that you might have no energy for, because coming out can so often lead to giving a lesson. Depending on where you are today, it might even lead to a heated political debate. That can add up to a lot of emotional labor and energy expenditure over time. In extreme circumstances, coming out with your person's pronoun might actually put you at risk. This can also be the case if your (trans) person has switched from *she/her* to *he/him* pronouns or vice versa and you encounter someone you already know.

I strongly believe that owning up to this humanness and walking beside your loved one as a coconspirator is your best strategy. Long term you're more likely to damage your relationship—and therefore your own well-being—if you maintain a lofty, unspeakable standard that burns you out and makes you resent your loved one than if you're both real about the ways in which the world does and does not facilitate well-being for trans people and our loved ones. Don't let real societal barriers manifest in your relationship as a disavowal that those barriers exist. They do exist.

Instead, do your best to be real and talk about when/where you need to do the work of coming out and when/where your person really doesn't have to know or care if this happens. For example, if you're two thousand miles away from home in a grocery store and someone strikes up a conversation, does your person *really* need you to whip out their gender-neutral pronouns? Maybe the answer is yes, but don't assume it is before you've had a pragmatic conversation. And don't wait until you're tired and feeling resentful to sit down together and have it.

Refer back to my set of gender needs prompts in Chapter 6 if you need help here.

Your Past Is Not Your Present

In Chapter 5 my linguist friend Lex Konnelly said something important about using a trans person's correct pronouns that I want to bring back and extend to other aspects of gender-friendliness. Namely, you have two opportunities to get it right: before you make a mistake and after you make a mistake. If you've gotten it wrong, you can notice and then enact the "good mistake" that you've learned about in this book: Say sorry, rephrase, and move on. For someone like me this can be almost as lovely as not making the mistake in the first place.

This simple and effective formula is best suited to small-scale mistakes, like pronoun errors, but I recognize that you might be coming to this book thinking about bigger moments, namely when you may have reacted in a gender-*un*friendly way to someone else's gender expression or to learning something new about someone else's gender identity. Maybe you feel like you really blew it when a trans person you know came out to you, for example, and maybe you actually did (one or both of these things may be true).

We are all harmed by rigid rules around gender when we enforce them on people we love who transgress the rules, whether or not we know we are being gender enforcers. In so doing, we hurt others, but in damaging the relationships we are part of, we also hurt ourselves. If this is where you are, I have two suggestions.

1. First, I want you to do the hard work of leaning into the feelings that welled up in that moment, which could be something like confusion, remorse, or even grief. Recognize that these feelings are in part responses to how most of us have been taught about gender: what is right and what is wrong. Own up to your responsibility for hurting someone you care about, but also notice that you are hurting, and lay a share of

the blame on the ways in which gender was working in the space and time of your bad encounter. If rigidity and separateness didn't characterize the big two gender categories, our responses to each other would always be gender friendly. We react in a context, and gender is part of that context. This suggestion is about applying your gender expertise in a practice of mustering compassion for yourself.

2. My second suggestion is about rebuilding or repairing a relationship in which you have done this harm. If, for example, you reacted badly to someone you love when they came out to you as transgender or expressed gender in a way that went against your gendered expectations for them, there are things you can do:

   - You can communicate what you now understand about why you reacted that way: that you were participating, whether you knew it or not, in sending the kind of harmful message that trans and gender-nonconforming people receive all the time. You can share this understanding with the person, adding that you take responsibility for participating in this harm and you are now working hard on educating yourself so that you can do better.

   - And, as is a consistent theme throughout this book, you can tend to that relationship as best as you can. Your person might need time and space, and in that situation the gender-friendly thing to do is to let them know, with love and patience, that you will be there if (and hopefully when) they are ready to come back and talk to you about it. But don't push, and accept a no when it is given even if this hurts (in which case processing that hurt is important to do, but away from this person).

To sum up, by saying "your past is not your present," I'm inviting you to look over your shoulder to that moment with that (odds are) transgender person who you didn't welcome very well, or at all, and give yourself permission to move forward. You can't get into a time machine, go backward, and undo what happened in the past. The important thing is that you're here now, reading this book and growing your understanding of gender, how to be more gender friendly, and how to make changes that will benefit people who you might not have engaged in the best way before you began this work. If this is you, know that this is your second opportunity to get it right, and move forward in a good way now.

Find Your Own Gender Happiness

It's easy to dwell on gender as a source of harm, whether it's the harm people do to others or the harm we do to ourselves with impossible expectations, self-surveillance, and self-punishment. As an educator, sometimes I've focused too much on the harm that gender can do. I've learned to balance discussions of gender harm with discussions of gender happiness from my colleague and education scholar Karleen Pendleton Jiménez.

What is your gender happiness? What do you love about your gender? Is your most beloved object, tradition, or pastime "stereotypical" for a person of your gender identity? Have you come to believe that you shouldn't be happy about it because it's stereotypical? I hope not. There is absolutely nothing wrong with being a woman who strongly identifies as a woman and loves all things associated with femininity, or being a man who strongly identifies as a man and loves all things associated with masculinity. Many transgender people feel this way, and many cisgender people feel this way too.

Gender itself isn't good or bad. It's placing *value* on some ways of doing gender that can get us into trouble, particularly when we decide that some ways are better than others. Badness happens when gender expectations are rigidly, uniformly enforced on everyone, or when we don't tolerate momentary or lifelong changes in how people around us do gender. Having been on different sides of gender throughout my life, I've experienced the harm of rigid gender expectations for girls and the harm of rigid gender expectations for masculine people in my own queer and transgender communities. I don't want to replace rigid rules with other rigid rules, or elevate gender nonconformity or being trans above all other gender pathways.

However, there *is* one thing about being transgender that I'd like to mainstream. When I meet other trans people, I'm often inspired by the fierce love that so many of us have for our gender. Many of us have fought harder for our gender than we can possibly express. And I want everyone—cisgender and transgender—to find the kind of happiness in your gender that I have come to find in mine. The more you make friends with your gender and come to name and honor it, the easier it'll be to keep on going in the gender-friendly work when you feel tired, unsupported, or unrecognized. In other words, if you can articulate what you love and take pride in about being your particular kind of man, woman, boy, or girl, or some or none of these, you won't fall into the trap of wondering whether someone else's gender is worth the trouble it sometimes takes to do your gender-friendly best. You'll *know* it is, and you'll remember that gender-friendliness is a project for everyone, yourself included. Because, who knows—you might not do gender this way forever. Wouldn't it be great if you cultivated a gender-friendly space around you so that others were ready to welcome *your* changing relationship with gender?

How to Debunk False Arguments Against Gender-Friendly Change

From where I sat while writing the first edition, *explicit* gender-diversity intolerance was on the wane, whether toward transgender people or the more general changes that come with the new gender culture. The pendulum is swinging backward as this edition goes to press. A new set of arguments has arisen that seeks to delegitimize gender-friendly shifts but come dressed in intellectual garb. Today they are becoming increasingly mainstream in the US and, less so, in Canada. Many but not all people voicing these arguments wouldn't say they're necessarily anti-transgender in their views or values, just skeptical of the societal changes they are seeing. The trouble is that researchers have soundly debunked each argument I'll discuss next, over and over again.

That said, I believe that someone who voices one of these arguments shouldn't be automatically discounted because trying on a talking point doesn't mean they're entirely opposed to the existence and well-being of transgender people, or to the freedom of people to do gender in their own way. Someone might just be repeating what they saw on TV or online and not realize that they're parroting misinformation or making a space decidedly gender *un*friendly. This is why it's important to be able to correct the record and offer accurate information when you're trying to invite other people into the work, which I'll address at length at the end of this chapter. Here, I'll give you some accessible strategies for responding to some common

 HEY! WHERE DID THE OTHER ARGUMENTS GO?

Just as gender is always changing, sadly so are the arguments against gender-friendly change. Other arguments that have arisen in the past include: people trying to equate being transracial with being transgender (nope), or claiming they could go to jail just for saying the wrong pronoun (they can't), or arguing that agreeing to use one person's neo-pronouns (e.g., xe/xem—see Chapter 4) means you'll someday have to learn a different pronoun for every trans person you meet (it doesn't). These arguments have faded over time due to educational work by trans people and our supporters, and the general population's growing familiarity with trans people in everyday life.

And the work continues. Unfortunately, there will always be new arguments cropping up, so stay vigilant and access sources authored by credible experts. In my most optimistic moments, I secretly hope this section—and indeed this entire book—will someday no longer be needed. As my dad used to say, my job is putting myself out of a job. Yes, please! I have several neglected hobbies.

arguments, each of which is based on misconception and/or misinformation. You can also check out and share the infographics I cocreated as part of the No Big Deal Campaign, free and downloadable under a Creative Commons license at www.nbdcampaign.ca.

The "But Grammar!" Argument

People whose pronouns are singular *they/them* or who are committed to using someone's correct *they/them* pronouns often hear this objection: "But it's grammatically incorrect!" Many of us were taught to match our nouns and pronouns in number and (binary) gender, but the English language is changing, and it's now considered acceptable to use *they/them* to refer to a singular known person. In my experience, people argue that singular *they* is grammatically incorrect when they feel like they're having to make more of an effort than usual to speak a language they've been speaking since birth. In fact, I've noticed that some people who speak English as an additional language have an easier time using my pronouns if their first language also has gender-neutral pronouns. I often hear the grammar argument from English speakers who are voracious readers and good writers. This is kind of the "smart people" objection, not because people are smarter for saying it, but because it sounds smart and people get away with it.

But never fear! The grammar argument is false. In Chapter 4 my linguist friends Bronwyn and Lex refuted it on several grounds. Here are all of their learned rebuttals in one place:

- Language changes all the time, but most of the time we aren't conscious of this happening. Historically, when people have been conscious of language changes as they take place, this has sparked controversy. But a thing isn't grammatically wrong just because it's controversial.
- Saying "they" for one person has been grammatically correct in English for centuries. What feels new is using it for someone you know.

- For linguists, something is "grammatically correct" when speakers of a language do it. English speakers use singular *they* for this purpose; therefore, it is correct.
- Having to work at saying a thing doesn't mean it's grammatically incorrect.
- Disagreeing with singular *they* won't make it go away. The change in its use to include a known person has taken hold, and it's inevitable.

The final thing I'll say about the grammar argument is that it's a stubborn one. When I find myself in a conversation where the grammar misconception persists even after I've refuted it with linguistic evidence, I shift gears because it's been revealed as a not-actually-grammatical objection, despite appearances. Maybe this is because, as I said earlier, the objector is someone highly literate who's also highly uncomfortable in situations where they don't know what to say. Learning to say "they are" for one person takes some effort where speaking is usually effort*less*, and can feel awkward. If you find yourself here in a conversation, I suggest that you, too, shift gears and empathize with the anxiety inherent in trying this out and making mistakes in the beginning. It's awkward, and that's okay. The awkwardness dissipates with time. This is all part of normalizing mistakes and calling people in instead of out.

However, the grammar misconception might persist despite all linguistic evidence to the contrary because of deep-seated gender-*un*friendliness lurking underneath a grammar argument. Someone who holds anti-trans views may feel like their views aren't shared by others or might know that acting on their views might be discriminatory in a particular context, like their workplace for example. Talking about grammar may be a way to express something, but not *the* thing. If someone is stubborn about grammar, and you think this is why, it can be useful to bracket grammar altogether and use the advice I shared in previous chapters on setting boundaries and using pronoun (etc.) work-arounds. After all, holding views and sharing

RESPONDING TO AN (IN)CORRECTION

Because the grammar argument is still common despite being incorrect, you might run into a situation where someone in a position of authority "corrects" your written use of singular *they* (English speakers are far less likely to notice singular *they* in speech unless gender is at issue—refer back to the Chapter 4 sidebars). Here, I'm talking about people who can compel you to change or edit something you have written, like a teacher or a supervisor. This often looks like getting a document sent back with *they* changed to *she* or *he*, and maybe even *with points taken off for "poor" grammar!* *shakes fist*

This situation is challenging because the correcting person is probably confident that they're right and you're wrong, and isn't used to receiving any pushback on their grammar supremacy. If you've used singular *they* because it's someone's correct gender pronoun, this is an equity issue and therefore nonnegotiable. It might even be covered under a policy of some kind in your institution, if applicable. However, it's best not to start there, but to approach the (in)corrector in a way that offers a chance to recognize their error: "I see that you changed this, which means that I need to be clearer about why I had *they* in that spot. X's pronouns are *they/them*, and so the text must remain that way in order to be accurate. Do you have suggestions on how I can make that clearer?" If the objection persists, we're not in grammar territory anymore, and it might be a moment to call in some help from whoever is tasked with addressing equity issues where you are.

If you used singular *they* in a more general sense and *not* because you were referring to a *they/them* user, I suggest a respectful approach in which you offer that it's okay to disagree, but that agreeing to disagree reflects the reality that singular *they* is both a change in progress *and* correct in English. You might also offer some points made by Lex and Bronwyn in Chapter 4 as compelling nuggets of information (not ironclad laws). Diplomacy is key, especially if you are in a subordinate position to the (in)corrector.

them in the public marketplace of ideas isn't the same as, say, being a medical receptionist who misgenders patients on purpose.

The "Free Speech" or "Compelled Speech" Argument

This argument holds that legal gender identity and gender expression protections threaten "freedom of speech" rights. The free speech argument usually goes like this: "I don't believe the government should be able to tell me which words I have to say." This argument is false because, well, it just is. The state does not tell people what words they *must* say, by law and under threat of sanction. Human rights laws typically require people to *not* say particular words in particular contexts, as with laws against hate speech, but do not say what words constitute hate speech.

There is no law, and there will never be, that *requires a person to say they/them* when referring to me. However, in Canada and in many US jurisdictions, there are laws that require my employer to provide me with a workplace free from gender identity and gender expression discrimination, and to take action when it happens. In Canada, people have successfully brought human rights complaints to tribunals alleging that their workplace, school, or vital public service is a discriminatory environment because people there have repeatedly and intentionally *said the wrong gender pronouns* for them (etc.). An example is *Nelson v. Goodberry Restaurant Group Ltd. dba Buono Osteria and others* in British Columbia in 2021, where Jessie Nelson (a nonbinary person) was awarded damages from their employer who did not take action to address the misgendering they were experiencing. The employer even fired Nelson when they acted out their frustration with their misgendering manager. Critically, the misgendering manager *did not have to pay Nelson any damages himself*—the discriminatory climate created by his unaddressed behavior was his employer's problem.

I appreciate Alberta lawyer Joel Fairbrother's take on the case, writing that "People very often confuse the notion of their right to have an opinion with their right to do whatever they want. The manager in this case obviously had an opinion that Jesse [sic] Nelson's nonbinary gender was nonsense. He was (and is) entitled to that opinion. What he was not entitled to do was to deliberately address Jesse [sic] Nelson using pronouns they asked him not to use. That is discrimination." If the manager had simply *not misgendered* Nelson, and there was no other discrimination, the case may not have gone to tribunal at all.

My friend Allison Burgess, the acting executive director of equity, diversity, and inclusion at the University of Toronto, suggests a work-around if someone refuses to use another person's correct gender pronouns and invokes the free speech argument. You can affirm that, no, they don't *have* to say that person's exact pronouns, but they still may not refer to that person with the wrong pronouns. How they handle that in everyday speech is up to them. I suggest referring them to the pronoun work-arounds I offer in Chapter 5. These include but are not limited to saying someone's (chosen) name instead of any pronoun.

The "It's Unfair for Trans Girls/Women to Play Sports!" Argument

Transgender men and transgender women have been competing in elite sports for decades. However, a grassroots movement against trans girls in high school sports has become a national platform plank of conservative Republicanism in the US. In April 2023, *The Independent* reported that twenty US states had banned trans women and girls from competing in women's or girls' school sports categories. In only a few cases were trans men and boys included in these "trans bans." This tells us something about assumptions regarding who "naturally" plays well versus who needs the "leg up" provided by separate sex categories (hint: not men). I know many cisgender women who find such blanket assumptions insulting, and I get why!

The substance of the "it's unfair for trans girls/women to play sports" argument is the fairness piece: that these girls/women

GENDER EXPRESSION HUMAN RIGHTS ARE FOR CISGENDER PEOPLE TOO

Gender identity human rights are, by definition, for transgender people, but gender expression human rights—where they exist in law—are conceivably for everybody. Gender expression discrimination is consistently being legally interpreted as, for example, other people *saying the wrong pronouns* either deliberately or consistently with no change over time *and* no action taken by the institution. My prediction: In the coming years, a cisgender boy being repeatedly and/or intentionally addressed with *she/her* pronouns at school because his gender expression is not typically masculine, or a cisgender woman being repeatedly and/or intentionally addressed with *he/him* pronouns in her workplace because her gender expression is not typically feminine, will be awarded damages from their school or employer, respectively, because they are found to have experienced unchecked gender expression discrimination. Here, then, is another debunking strategy for the "but free speech!" argument: that pronouns can actually be a tool for inflicting harm against any person—transgender or cisgender—because they are not neutral words.

necessarily have an advantage over other girls/women. Here are two common varieties of this argument and ways to speak back:

- "Transgender women dominate women's sports!" No, they don't. We just hear a *lot* about the occasional trans woman athlete who gets far enough to compete, despite all the odds stacked against her in sport and society. Becoming an elite athlete means money—often provided by supportive parents, which many trans youth still don't have—and years of preparation from childhood. But the 2019 Canadian Trans and Non-Binary Youth Health Survey found that only one in ten participated in a sport or other physical activity with a coach, and GLSEN's 2019 National School Climate Survey found that over half of the surveyed transgender students were prevented or discouraged from playing school sports. All this is to say that trans people are a minority in society, and trans elite athletes are a tiny minority within that. Focusing on the scant trans women athletes who have made it far enough is a choice, made by media chasing clicks and by anti-transgender voices, that has little to do with "fairness" in sports. Rather, this focus serves a broader anti-trans agenda that's becoming increasingly explicit in North America and around the world. Further, the assumption that a person assigned male at birth will win is incredibly sexist. Even in powerlifting, a sport rife with stereotypical assumptions about gender and strength, the first trans woman Olympian, Laurel Hubbard, didn't get near the podium in Tokyo 2020. However, I wager that the bare fact of her participation received more international news coverage than the entire sport of women's powerlifting in the history of sports journalism. Anybody remember the actual medalists? No? Hmm.

- "More testosterone gives an unfair advantage!" Lots to say here. First, everyone has testosterone, and even cisgender women's testosterone levels vary! Some women have more testosterone than the typical male-assigned person, and only a small number of these women are transgender—some are cisgender, and some are intersex (see Chapter 1). Across different sports and different events within the same sport, higher testosterone levels do not universally confer an advantage, and yet, anti-trans sports bans are universal. The International Olympic Committee, the world's highest-level sport governing body, places the burden on individual sport federations to *prove* advantage based on credible research—much research has been found inconclusive or biased—and not apply discriminatory blanket bans. The IOC also calls on federations to prevent harmful "sex testing," which is invasive and even traumatic for trans women and girls as well as cisgender women and girls targeted due to suspicions that they are trans. Lastly, the IOC acknowledges other "biological" advantages in elite-level competition, such as Olympic swimming champion Michael Phelps's body producing less than half the lactic acid of other athletes' bodies, meaning he can swim fast for longer periods of time. Phelps is celebrated for an *actual proven advantage*, and trans women athletes are being driven out of all competitive sports due to *unfounded perceptions of advantage*. Once again, we have to ask whether this argument is really about fairness in sports or just part of broader partisan efforts to keep transgender people out of public life. There is a lot more to say about the scientific and medical facts debunking this argument. I refer interested readers to Ali Durham Greey and Helen Jefferson Lenskyj's book *Justice for Trans Athletes: Challenges and Struggles*, and *Testosterone: An Unauthorized Biography* by Rebecca M. Jordan-Young and Katrina Karkazis.

Other Arguments

In addition to the arguments I've focused on debunking here, you might encounter other erroneous arguments about gender diversity and transgender people as you go about your gender-friendly work. You can speak back to these misconceptions using information in these chapters:

- Gender identity, including but not only in transgender people, cannot be changed via conversion therapy, socialization, or, in children and youth, peer pressure. (Chapter 3)
- Children are not receiving irreversible hormone therapies or gender-affirming surgeries. (Chapter 3)
- Many people who detransition do so because of a lack of support for their original transition or because they experienced

significant discrimination as a trans person, not because "they are not really transgender." (Chapter 3)

- There is no single definitive answer about *why* transgender people exist, just enduring evidence that we do across time and the world. (Chapter 3)
- Transgender people face a statistically disproportionate risk of violence and harassment in public gendered washrooms, and cisgender people do not. (Chapters 3 and 7)

There are many fine resources that can also help you debunk misconceptions when they arise where you are, and some are included in the bibliography.

Tips for Taking a Leadership Role with Others

Changing the way you participate in gender can be lonely for many reasons. Of course, if you aren't *actually* going it alone, you're less likely to feel isolated. It's lovely to have other people who share your commitment to welcoming gender diversity instead of snuffing it out. If you're the first person in your family, friend group, workplace, or school who's shifting toward more gender-friendly language and practice, it can help both you and the work if you take a leadership role by inviting others into making these shifts too. Here are some suggestions.

Expect Good Things from Others

Gender-friendliness isn't about perfection. It's a commitment to doing your best to keep gender open around you and meet the stated (and sometimes unstated) gender-related needs of the people in your life. It's about a willingness to receive gentle reminders and corrections with grace and good humor. There is gender-friendliness all around you, even in places that you wouldn't expect. Last summer my partner Tama and I were at a car dealership in a Toronto suburb, and when I gently asked the salesman not to call us "ladies," he responded by telling us about this TV show he started watching (*Billions*) and its "gender-neutral" character who uses *they/them* pronouns. Basically, he was letting me know that he was okay with my deal in an awkward yet kindly way, and he moved on, having studiously avoided using any pronouns for me the entire time we'd been talking.

This story is just one example where I've stated my gender needs and been met in a good way. I keep being pleasantly surprised by complete strangers, and I hear more and more stories about this kind of thing from other trans people too. It needs to be said, however, that we were potential customers, or people not to be alienated due to our privilege. I don't know what would have happened if we'd met on equal footing in his private life. But I choose to proceed as if people aren't going to meet me in a bad way unless I have evidence that they will. This isn't a nice thing I do for others; it's a self-care strategy. I've found this to be far less draining than embodying the opposite expectation: that people are going to let me down. They most certainly have. But my posture toward a new person, to whatever extent I can manage on a particular day, is that they're somebody who will show up well.

I know this story was about *being* a trans person, but I'd like to extend its implications to my readers who might not be trans or gender nonconforming but are trying to practice gender-friendliness: This can be easier if you embody the expectation that other people *will* meet you in a good way when you're acting on what you've learned in this book (and elsewhere). When you correct someone's pronoun usage, ask a waiter to stop with the "ladies," or bring up bathroom signage in your workplace, try to embody the expectation that you'll be met with grace. Model this expectation with your facial expression, body language, and tone. In my experience, this modeling can help others respond to you in the same way.

Model Good Mistakes

In Chapter 5, I suggested that mistakes are inevitable, and that you shouldn't aim for "no mistakes" when you're making gender-friendly language changes or trying to use someone's new or new-to-you pronoun. There are only good mistakes and bad mistakes. As you know by now, a good one looks like this: quick sorry, rephrase, move on, all with a neutral tone. A bad mistake draws so much attention to the issue that a person might not correct anyone else in that space ever again. The trouble is that you might be the only person where you are who has read this book and who knows this formula.

It's a good idea, then, to model good mistakes for the people around you. When you get someone's pronouns wrong, make sure you do the whole "sorry, rephrase, and move on" routine. If you do this enough, others will see you do it and try to emulate. You can also explicitly draw attention to this strategy when you do it, or bring it up later on in a conversation if you need an example. When someone else makes a mistake and catches themself in front of you, respond like it's no big deal and try to deter exaggerated apologies if they arise by gently drawing attention back to the issue or conversation at hand and away from the apologies.

Last thing: If you're the person leading the gender-friendly charge in your space, know that your mistakes will be scrutinized. This is unfortunate because it increases pressure on you to not make a mistake, which is bogus because it's impossible. So, if you're ever targeted by someone for your own mistake—in a "haha" or "aha" kind of way—a good response is to normalize mistake making: It happens. The goal isn't to make no mistakes because that's impossible; the goal is to help each other make a sustainable shift over time. Try your best not to let this kind of response derail the patience and compassion that you're modeling for others around you.

Let Go of Needing to Know Everything

This tip comes from my dad, star of a much-loved Chapter 6 sidebar where I shared how he changed "Miss America" to "Person America" so he could keep singing the theme song when I emerged in the morning during visits home. In the years since the first edition, I often elaborate on this story and say more about Dad and how he made me feel: as if every time we were together or talking on the phone it was the highlight of his life. And he was my cheerleader throughout the process of making *Gender: Your Guide*. But you know what? I don't know for sure if he read the thing.

I don't know because I'm pretty sure Dad would have failed the final exam. I'm sure he wasn't clear on the differences between me, a trans man, and a gender-fluid person, or could explain the differences among gender identity, gender expression, and sexual orientation. Nevertheless, my dad did four things after I came out as nonbinary that made all the difference in the world:

- Dad knew that not being referred to as a girl or woman or female was important to me, even if he wasn't clear exactly why all the time, so he just didn't do it.
- Dad knew that saying *they/them* for me was something I needed him to do, so he used my pronouns to the best of his ability, often caught his own mistakes, and, when I let him know he'd slipped up, was nice about it.
- Dad followed my lead. I'll give you an example. He had a lively social network in the semirural community where my parents lived after retirement. Dad bought things or borrowed things, gave or received advice on projects, and always stuck around for a chat. One time I was with him, and we pulled up to an acquaintance's home. The guy heard us pull up, walked down the driveway, and clocked me. I felt his intensive scrutiny on my face and torso like a heat lamp: a familiar feeling to many trans folks. To Dad, he said, "Why doesn't your son get out of the car and say hello to me?" all the while staring through the windshield like a hawk. Dad clearly wanted to stay and chat, but I just said that I didn't want to. No problem. Dad got out alone, quickly completed his business, and we were on our way. There was no postmortem questioning and no defensiveness about the person's intentions. We just got on with our day.

- Lastly, and perhaps most importantly, Dad didn't moan or complain about doing any of this. He probably felt sometimes like it was weird, or a lot to remember, or even unreasonable. But if he did, I never heard about it.

After all that, here's the tip: Let go of needing to know for sure what all is going on with someone before doing your best, and encourage others to do the same. You might never fully understand the why, but you can move forward with the how. This is worlds better than *telling* someone you get it. It's *showing* them that you are on their team. And if this someone is your kid, you are doing the best thing you can possibly do.

Celebrate Others' Efforts

Don't forget to notice and even celebrate (if appropriate) other people's small changes, and try not to limit your responses to correcting mistakes. If you hear the receptionist at work direct a person to "the bathrooms," including the gender-neutral one, give that receptionist a high five (after the person has left). I get that this is a rather extrovert-friendly suggestion (my bias), but I hope you get the idea: that positive feedback, even for small things, begets more gender-friendly efforts. You invite other people into the work when you model realistic expectations based on their starting place.

In my experience, the opposite is also true. Only ever correcting and even shaming people for their mistakes makes them not want to learn or make an effort, and can promote apathy—that they shouldn't even try—or even hostility toward "those people," which is counterproductive. While I am here for being too tired to take care of other people's feelings sometimes, it's a reality that people who are called out too hard or too often just shut down. Having patience and showing appreciation for small changes is a great way to invite others in.

Don't Tell Other People Who They Are, and See What Happens

As you've learned throughout the book, we all have skin in the gender game, and we all have latent gender expertise that can be put to use in making more gender-friendly spaces. Remember, being gender friendly can help you be kinder to yourself when you don't meet lofty gender expectations. Sending out these signals can also lead to new connections, including with people you already know. This is because when we change how we relate to others around us, we change relationships. When you become someone who doesn't unintentionally tell other people who they are or how they should feel (look back at Chapter 7 for examples), people notice. Over time, this noticing can lead to conversations where you share your rationale with others, which can in turn lead them to see the value, for everyone, in being gender friendly.

I'll give you an example. We don't often recognize how names are part of gender expression and not just a generic preference. In fact, many cisgender people have strong preferences about the names they get called by others. What image springs to mind when you picture a Chrissy versus a Christina, a Jen versus a Jennifer, a Mike versus a Michael, or a Teddy versus an Edward? The first names are all short versions or diminutives of the second names, and each one sends a different message. I'm not saying any name is better or worse but illustrating how gender is a lot about messaging. How does each person appear in your mind, and what kinds of things does that imaginary person participate in? What kind of femininity and/or masculinity do you associate with that person?

Remember that each of us alters our gender expression as we move among the different spaces in our lives, and many people get called different names at work versus among friends, for example. People I know are often surprised when I remember how their unique name is spelled or when I gently correct someone who has defaulted to an unwelcome diminutive of their name. Here's the point: This isn't "just being polite"; it's a part of *my* gender-friendly practice. As a nonbinary person, I know how important little words can be. And, thinking back to my discussion of gender happiness, for me remembering others' needs never feels like a chore because I know how important it is. It's actually a pleasure to offer someone this form of care and feel its positive impact on our relationship. The same goes for any effort I make to convey to others, with my spoken language, body language, facial expression, and tone, that I am paying attention and doing my best to see the person they are putting out there.

Last Word

In working your way through this book, you've developed a tool kit for navigating and welcoming all the ways that gender is lived, wherever you are. I've also shown you some tools you already had: experiences and abilities that become tools when you begin to name and notice how gender plays out in your own life and in the lives of people around you, whether transgender or cisgender. In fact, I wanted to write this book because two related phenomena come together in the new gender culture but aren't usually addressed together:

1. Trans people are increasingly coming out and being visible in our everyday lives.
2. There is a growing consensus that enforcing rigid gender expectations isn't worth the harm and unhappiness this can cause, for transgender and cisgender people alike.

In my own field of education, for example, there is a research community that studies stress, anxiety, and forms of self-harm among children and youth, and another research community that studies the negative school experiences of queer and/or transgender children and youth. Only rarely do we see connections drawn between these two areas of study, which might center the daily pressure young people feel to conform to rigid gender rules and expectations, which is also felt by people across the lifespan.

A key theme across the book's chapters is that there's much more that brings us together than keeps us apart, in terms of how we live with and sometimes in spite of gender, its joys, and its challenges. This is why I wrote this book for everyone and why I invite you to think about how gender is working out for you, whoever you are, as a starting place for thinking about how it might be working out for other people around you. I offer *Gender: Your Guide, 2nd Edition* in the hope that it can help foster more gender joy, in all the ways this joy can and will be experienced, and less gender harm. This can happen when people like you and me step up and step into this together.

CODA:

To the Trans Person Whose Person Is Reading This Book

Who Am I and Why Did I Write This Book?

Self-Advocacy Tips and Resources

Hi there! I'm so glad you've come here for this special message. Of course, not everyone who reads this book has a particular trans person in mind, but some readers most certainly do. This could be you. If so, throughout *Gender: Your Guide, 2nd Edition* I've tried to provide the reader with tools to meet *your* needs (but not only), and so it's only right that I introduce myself.

I include this coda because my own experiences undoubtedly led me to some choices (and away from others) in how I wrote and illustrated the content. I wanted to share a little bit about myself so you know where I'm coming from. I've shared a lot in the book already, but I know that you might not read it, which is a-okay. I also wanted to make some space to center trans and gender-nonconforming people in a book that's otherwise geared toward those who might not know very much about gender diversity and the issues many trans people face.

Who Am I and Why Did I Write This Book?

This book is the descendant of *They Is My Pronoun*, a blog I started in 2012 at TheyIsMyPronoun.com (now archived) with a practical and inviting address to someone who might be encountering trans people and our language needs for the first time. When it was first published in 2018, *Gender: Your Guide* was one of the only—if not *the* only—books about gender diversity that was *prescriptive*, or that actually tells people what to do. Through my educational and advocacy work around trans issues, and my work with beginning teachers, I've learned about the importance of a starting place. There are many people out there who don't wish trans or gender-nonconforming people any harm whatsoever, or who might even wish us well but lack the first clue about what any of this even means. After all, most people think they haven't met one of us, and only some of them are correct.

I've often reflected on why my contribution to trans advocacy has been working in this beginner space, and I think that I'm able to do so because of the resources I have that many trans people do not. I'm lucky to have a supportive family, for starters, which as we both know is a key determinant of trans people's (and specifically trans youth's) life chances. I'm also privileged in the sense of my social position, in that I'm white and a university professor. I'm a settler who was born and raised on unceded Musqueam, Squamish, and Tsleil-Waututh territory, and today I live and work on traditional Anishinaabe and Haudenosaunee territory. I have lived most of my life in major Canadian cities, which are relatively good places to be a trans person, at least in terms of community presence, human rights protections, and supportive policies. I'm nonbinary and have had *they/them* pronouns since 2011. I'm also on the masculine side, which means that I don't face some of the issues that femme nonbinary (etc.) people experience, inside and outside of trans spaces, or what transfeminine people and transgender women experience.

This all adds up to a particular perspective on gender diversity and transgender issues, which has undoubtedly shaped the book. I've done my best to round out my own perspective by including the scholarship and voices of others, and I hope that what I've offered will be useful to you and the people around you.

That said, it's a given that some of it will need tweaking to make it align with your own situation. My goal is *not* to provide the definitive account of what to do, for all people, for all time. Rather, I'll feel like the book is successful if *you* can have a next-level conversation with your person about what needs tweaking here in order to meet your needs, beginning from and not ending with the baseline knowledge they've acquired from reading it.

Self-Advocacy Tips and Resources

Over many years of supporting and learning from other trans people, I've developed an approach to self-advocacy that centers on relationships. I believe the capacity to meet trans people's needs with grace and goodwill will grow if we attend to the relationships in which we are coming out and making an ask. What we are asking for does take effort, and it's effort that we *absolutely* need them to expend when we're not there, when we will not notice or appreciate the expenditure, and when we are not there to take the lead. With all of this in mind, here are my top four self-advocacy tips for a transgender-spectrum person thinking about coming out to and/or making an ask of someone else in their life.

- Think of yourself as your person's teacher. And what makes a good teacher? No pop quizzes, clear and realistic expectations, not humiliating someone if they don't know the answer, tailoring instruction and assignments to students' interests and aptitudes, and more. What other "good teacher" characteristics can you come up with? Take each of these characteristics and think about how you could apply them—to whatever extent possible—in conversations about your gender.

- See also Chapter 9 where I talk about how to invite others into the work alongside you, and the "other" in this book is typically cisgender. However, many of those tips also apply to self-advocacy.
- Be ready to give practical and actionable instructions, with examples, on exactly what you are asking them to do. The person might have very little idea of what it means to meet the needs you just shared with them, and might be just starting to notice how and how often gender becomes relevant in their daily lives when they have to talk about you to others (etc.). When, where, and with whom are you asking them to do what, exactly? Are there boundaries around your requests? Unfortunately, anger and resentment can be ways that humans cope with feeling like they don't know what to do or are not in control. The more precise you can be, the less likely they'll get stressed out and act on their stress by pivoting to unhelpful emotional responses.
  - In Chapter 6, I share some exploratory questions I use in workshops with trans and/or nonbinary youth to help them take stock of their needs in order to clearly communicate them to others, which might be useful.
  - See also: https://theyismypronoun.wordpress.com/2014/09/06/start-with-affirmation-coming-out-as-a-gnp-user-or-gender-non-normative-person-to-a-friend-with-little-or-no-knowledge-of-gender-issues
  - See also: https://theyismypronoun.wordpress.com/2015/08/25/151
- When we make our needs known and make an ask of another person, this happens in the context of a particular relationship and all the previous experiences we have had together, not in a vacuum. When you're thinking about how and when to come out or to make an ask of someone in your life, reflect on and hopefully tend to this relationship. If you haven't checked in for a while, check in. If you haven't spent time, spend time. If

you've been hurtful, authentically make amends. Do your best to build or build up the foundation so that when you call this person in, you are doing so in a context of mutual care. I get that this might not be possible, for many reasons. But if it is, it's worthwhile to tend before and after you make the ask.

- See also: https://theyismypronoun.wordpress
  .com/2015/09/12/why-its-hard-sometimes-resistance-to-
  pronoun-change-can-have-nothing-to-do-with-pronouns
- See also: https://theyismypronoun.wordpress
  .com/2014/09/06/youre-being-disrespectful-are-negative-
  parent-reactions-to-gnp-always-about-gender
- See also: https://theyismypronoun.wordpress
  .com/2014/07/17/fearing-partner-rejection-because-of-a-
  gender-neutral-pronoun-request

- The people around you know a lot about gender and how it works, but they might not know that they know. They might not know how to draw connections between their own experiences navigating gender expectations and yours. Worse, they might feel like they can't because they've been trained to think that trans people are from outer space. We aren't. So, when you have conversations with your person about your gender, it's helpful to draw connections to their own gendered experiences, joys, and hurts so that they can more easily feel their way into what you are sharing with them. What do they love about being their gender that you can draw on when talking about what you love about being your gender? How have they struggled with the gendered rules for their category, and how can you relate their experiences to your struggles?
  - See also Chapter 2, where I suggest some ways for the reader to locate their own gender expertise.

- New in the second edition! Chapter 8 now features a fifth step in my action plan toward gender-friendly change: Make a Power Move. Here I talk about how to prepare for and conduct yourself in meetings with people who wield power (the example is a trans kid and their supporting adult meeting with the school principal). These suggestions were developed with a group of experts in gender, education, and law as part of my research project about education policy on gender identity and gender expression human rights in Ontario, Canada. Regardless of where you are, this section may help you to take on the task of getting your human rights respected and, crossing my fingers, your needs met. Our website www.gegi.ca has more information to help you self-advocate, even if you don't live in Canada.

Thank you for reading, and I hope there is something in the book that proves useful to you or to someone you know. I hope to see you sometime when I'm out on the road. If you like, visit me at LeeAirton.com. I'd love to hear from you.

Bibliography

Ahmed, S. (2017). *Living a feminist life*. Duke University Press. https://doi.org/10.2307/j.ctv11g9836

Beemyn, G., & Rankin, S. (2011). *The lives of transgender people*. Columbia University Press.

Blackless, M., Charuvastra, A., Derryck, A., Fausto-Sterling, A., Lauzanne, K., & Lee, E. (2000). How sexually dimorphic are we? Review and synthesis. *American Journal of Human Biology*, *12*(2), 151–166. https://doi.org/bttkh4

Boellstorff, T., Cabral, M., Cárdenas, M., Cotten, T., Stanley, E. A., Young, K., & Aizura, A. Z. (2014). Decolonizing transgender: A roundtable discussion. *Transgender Studies Quarterly*, *1*(3), 419–439. https://doi.org/10.1215/23289252-2685669

Bowles, H. (2020, November 13). Playtime with Harry Styles. *Vogue*. www.vogue.com/article/harry-styles-cover-december-2020

Branigin, A. (2022, July 27). A record number of trans and nonbinary people are running for office. *The Washington Post*. www.washingtonpost.com/nation/2022/07/27/trans-nonbinary-candidates-2022

Bruni, F. (2008, October 7). Old gender roles with your dinner? *The New York Times*. www.nytimes.com/2008/10/08/dining/08gend.html

Burga, S. (2023, March 14). Florida bills would ban teachers from calling students pronouns that differ from their biological sex. *Time*. https://time.com/6262797/florida-school-bill-ban-student-pronouns

Camilliere, S., Izes, A., Leventhal, O., & Grodner, D. (2021). *They* is changing: Pragmatic and grammatical factors that license singular *they*. *Proceedings of the Annual Meeting of the Cognitive Science Society, 43*, 1,542–1,548. https://escholarship.org/uc/item/3tc9s9b0

Cavanagh, S. L. (2010). *Queering bathrooms: Gender, sexuality, and the hygienic imagination*. University of Toronto Press.

CKNW Kids' Fund. (n.d.) *Pink shirt day*. www.pinkshirtday.ca/about

Clearfield, M. W., & Nelson, N. M. (2006). Sex differences in mothers' speech and play behavior with 6-, 9-, and 14-month-old infants. *Sex Roles, 54*(1–2), 127–137. https://doi.org/10.1007/s11199-005-8874-1

Colapinto, J. (2000). *As nature made him: The boy who was raised as a girl*. Harper Perennial.

Coleman, E., Radix, A. E., Bouman, W. P., Brown, G. R., de Vries, A. L. C., Deutsch, M. B., Ettner, R., Fraser, L., Goodman, M., Green, J., Hancock, A. B., Johnson, T. W., Karasic, D. H., Knudson, G. A., Leibowitz, S. F., Meyer-Bahlburg, H. F. L., Monstrey, S. J., Motmans, J., Nahata, L., ... Arcelus, J. (2022). Standards of Care for the Health of Transgender and Gender Diverse People, Version 8. *International Journal of Transgender Health, 23*(S1), S1–S259. https://doi.org/10.1080/26895269.2022.2100644

Colker, R. (2017). *Sexual orientation, gender identity, and the law in a nutshell*. West Academic Publishing.

Corbett, G. G. (2013). Sex-based and non-sex-based gender systems. In M. S. Dryer & M. Haspelmath (Eds.), *The world atlas of language structures online*. Max Planck Institute for Evolutionary Anthropology. http://wals.info/chapter/31

Department of Justice Canada. (2021). *Proposed changes to Canada's Criminal Code relating to conversion therapy*. www.justice.gc.ca/eng/csj-sjc/pl/ct-tc/index.html

Dreger, A. D., & Herndon, A. M. (2009). Progress and politics in the intersex rights movement: Feminist theory in action. *GLQ: A Journal of Lesbian and Gay Studies, 15*(2), 199–224. https://doi.org/10.1215/10642684-2008-134

Ekins, R., & King, D. (2006). *The transgender phenomenon*. SAGE Publications. https://doi.org/10.4135/9781446220917

Ellingworth, J., & Ho, S. (2021, August 2). *Laurel Hubbard, 1st openly transgender Olympic weightlifter, competes in Tokyo*. CBC Sports. www.cbc.ca/sports/olympics/summer/weightlifting/laurel-hubbard-1st-openly-transgender-weightlifting-olympian-1.6126764

Ellison, M. A., Hotamisligil, S., Lee, H., Rich-Edwards, J. W., Pang, S. C., & Hall, J. E. (2005). Psychosocial risks associated with multiple births resulting from assisted reproduction. *Fertility and Sterility, 83*(5), 1,422–1,428. https://doi.org/10.1016/j.fertnstert.2004.11.053

Elsesser, K. (2023, July 2). Elon Musk deems "cis" a twitter slur—here's why it's is [*sic*] so polarizing. *Forbes*. www.forbes.com/sites/kimelsesser/2023/07/02/elon-musk-deems-cis-a-twitter-slurheres-why-its-is-so-polarizing/?sh=2d66250f4ac6

Erickson-Schroth, L. (Ed.). (2022). *Trans bodies, trans selves: A resource by and for transgender communities* (2nd ed.). Oxford University Press.

Fairbrother, J. (2022, February 21). *Employer discriminates regarding gender pronouns*. CanLII Connects. https://canliiconnects.org/en/commentaries/86988

Flores, A. R. (2015). Attitudes toward transgender rights: Perceived knowledge and secondary interpersonal contact. *Politics, Groups, and Identities, 3*(3), 398–416. https://doi.org/10.1080/21565503.2015 .1050414

Frohard-Dourlent, H., Dobson, S., Clark, B. A., Doull, M., & Saewyc, E. M. (2016). "I would have preferred more options": Accounting for non-binary youth in health research. *Nursing Inquiry, 24*(1). https://doi.org/10.1111/nin.12150

Gamson, J. (1998). Publicity traps: Television talk shows and lesbian, gay, bisexual, and transgender visibility. *Sexualities, 1*(1), 11–41. https://doi.org/10.1177/136346098001001002

Gardner, A. (2023, October 19). A complete breakdown of the J. K. Rowling transgender-comments controversy. *Glamour.* www.glamour.com/story/a-complete-breakdown-of-the-jk-rowling-transgender-comments-controversy

Geselowitz, G. (2017, July 12). Come to the bimah and read from the Torah! But first, what's your preferred gender pronoun? *Tablet.* www.tabletmag.com/scroll/240492/come-to-the-bimah-and-read-from-the-torah-but-first-whats-your-preferred-gender-pronoun

Gill-Peterson, J. (2018). *Histories of the transgender child.* University of Minnesota Press. https://doi.org/10.5749/j.ctv75d87g

Glover, J. K. (2016). Redefining realness? On Janet Mock, Laverne Cox, TS Madison, and the representation of transgender women of color in media. *Souls: A Critical Journal of Black Politics, Culture, and Society, 18*(2–4), 338–357. https://doi.org/10.1080/10999949.2016 .1230824

GLSEN. (2021). *LGBTQ students and school sports participation (research brief).* www.glsen.org/sites/default/files/2022-02/LGBTQ-Students-and-School-Sports-Participation-Research-Brief.pdf

Goldberg, S., & Rose, C. B. (Eds.). (2009). *And baby makes more: Known donors, queer parents, and our unexpected families.* Insomniac Press.

Greey, A. D., & Lenskyj, H. J. (Eds.). (2022). *Justice for trans athletes: Challenges and struggles.* Emerald Publishing. https://doi.org/10.1108/9781802629859

Grenier, É. (2022, November 15). How Canada would vote in a U.S. election. *The Writ.* www.thewrit.ca/p/how-canada-would-vote-in-a-us-election

Grinberg, E., & Stewart, D. (2017, March 7). *3 myths that shape the transgender bathroom debate.* CNN. www.cnn.com/2017/03/07/health/transgender-bathroom-law-facts-myths/index.html

Hässler, T., Glazier, J. J., & Olson, K. R. (2022). Consistency of gender identity and preferences across time: An exploration among cisgender and transgender children. *Developmental Psychology, 58*(11), 2,184–2,196. https://doi.org/10.1037/dev0001419

Herman, J. L. (2013). Gendered restrooms and minority stress: The public regulation of gender and its impact on transgender people's lives. *Journal of Public Management and Social Policy, 19*(1), 65–80. https://williamsinstitute.law.ucla.edu/wp-content/uploads/Restrooms-Minority-Stress-Jun-2013.pdf

Hesse, M. (2019, May 2). We celebrated Michael Phelps's genetic differences. Why punish Caster Semenya for hers? *The Washington Post.* www.washingtonpost.com/lifestyle/style/we-celebrated-michael-phelpss-genetic-differences-why-punish-caster-semenya-for-hers/2019/05/02/93d08c8c-6c2b-11e9-be3a-33217240a539_story.html

Human Rights Watch & interACT. (2017). *"I want to be like nature made me": Medically unnecessary surgeries on intersex children in the US.* www.hrw.org/report/2017/07/25/i-want-be-nature-made-me/medically-unnecessary-surgeries-intersex-children-us

Iantaffi, A., & Barker, M. J. (2017). *How to understand your gender.* Jessica Kingsley Publishers.

International Olympic Committee. (n.d.). *IOC framework on fairness, inclusion and non-discrimination on the basis of gender identity and sex variations.* https://stillmed.olympics.com/media/Documents/Beyond-the-Games/Human-Rights/IOC-Framework-Fairness-Inclusion-Non-discrimination-2021.pdf

Jarry, J. (2021, November 13). *The word "cisgender" has scientific roots.* McGill Office for Science and Society. www.mcgill.ca/oss/article/history-general-science/word-cisgender-has-scientific-roots

Jiménez, K. P. (2016). "I love Barbies...I am a boy": Gender happiness for social justice education. *Sex Education, 16*(4), 379–390. https://doi.org/10.1080/14681811.2015.1067195

Jordan-Young, R. M., & Karkazis, K. (2019). *Testosterone: An unauthorized biography.* Harvard University Press.

Karvunidis, J., & Langmuir, M. (2020, June 29). I started the "gender reveal party" trend. And I regret it. *The Guardian.* www.theguardian.com/lifeandstyle/2020/jun/29/jenna-karvunidis-i-started-gender-reveal-party-trend-regret

Katz, J. N. (1995). *The invention of heterosexuality.* Dutton Books.

Kesslen, B. (2019, January 20). *Ms., Mr. or Mx.? Nonbinary teachers embrace gender-neutral honorific.* NBC News. www.nbcnews.com/feature/nbc-out/ms-mr-or-mx-nonbinary-teachers-embrace-gender-neutral-honorific-n960456#

Kessler, S. J. (1998). *Lessons from the intersexed.* Rutgers University Press.

Kidd, K. M., Sequeira, G. M., Douglas, C., Paglisotti, T., Inwards-Breland, D. J., Miller, E., & Coulter, R. W. S. (2021). Prevalence of gender-diverse youth in an urban school district. *Pediatrics, 147*(6). https://doi.org/10.1542/peds.2020-049823

Kirkup, K. (2018). The origins of gender identity and gender expression in Anglo-American legal discourse. *University of Toronto Law Journal, 68*(1), 80–117. https://doi.org/10.3138/utlj.2017-0080

Konnelly, L., & Cowper, E. (2020). Gender diversity and morphosyntax: An account of singular they. *Glossa: a journal of general linguistics, 5*(1), 1–19. https://doi.org/10.5334/gjgl.1000

Lodge, C. (2023). Gender census 2023: Worldwide report. *Gender Census.* www.gendercensus.com/results/2023-worldwide

MacKinnon, K. R., Expósito-Campos, P., & Gould, W. A. (2023). Detransition needs further understanding, not controversy. *BMJ, 381.* https://doi.org/10.1136/bmj-2022-073584

MacKinnon, K. R., Gould, W. A., Ashley, F., Enxuga, G., Kia, H., & Ross, L. E. (2022). (De)transphobia: Examining the socio-politically driven gender minority stressors experienced by people who detransitioned. *Bulletin of Applied Transgender Studies, 1*(3–4), 235–259. https://doi.org/10.57814/8nd4-6a89

Mayo Clinic. (n.d.). *Polycystic ovary syndrome (PCOS).* www.mayoclinic.org/diseases-conditions/pcos/symptoms-causes/syc-20353439

Merriam-Webster. (2019, September). *Is it ever okay to say "themself"?* www.merriam-webster.com/words-at-play/themself

Merriam-Webster. (2017, September). *Mx.—A gender-neutral honorific.* www.merriam-webster.com/words-at-play/mx-gender-neutral-title

Merriam-Webster. (n.d.). *Words we're watching: "Nibling."* www.merriam-webster.com/words-at-play/words-were-watching-nibling

Meyer, E. J., Tilland-Stafford, A., & Airton, L. (2016). Transgender and gender-creative students in PK–12 schools: What we can learn from their teachers. *Teachers College Record, 118*(8), 1–50. https://doi.org/10.1177/016146811611800806

Montpetit, J., & Ward, L. (2022, October 20). *Scores of anti-trans candidates running in Ontario school board elections.* CBC News. www.cbc.ca/news/canada/ontario-school-board-trustee-investigation-1.6622705

Movement Advancement Project. (2023, October 4). *Nondiscrimination/LGBTQ youth: Bans on transgender people's use of bathrooms and facilities.* www.lgbtmap.org/img/maps/citations-bathroom-facilities-bans.pdf

Murchison, G. R., Agénor, M., Reisner, S. L., & Watson, R. J. (2019). School restroom and locker room restrictions and sexual assault risk among transgender youth. *Pediatrics, 143*(6). https://doi.org/10.1542/peds.2018-2902

Namaste, V. (2011). *Sex change, social change: Reflections on identity, institutions, and imperialism* (2nd ed.). Canadian Scholars' Press.

National Center for Transgender Equality. (2023, February 28). *Get the facts: The truth about transition-related care for transgender youth.* https://transequality.org/blog/get-the-facts-the-truth-about-transition-related-care-for-transgender-youth

Nelson v. Goodberry Restaurant Group Ltd. dba Buono Osteria and others, 2021 BCHRT 137. www.bchrt.bc.ca/shareddocs/decisions/2021/sep/137_Nelson_v_Goodberry_Restaurant_Group_Ltd_dba_Buono_Osteria_and_others_2021_BCHRT_137.pdf

Ng, T. (2023, February 21). Raising kids in a gender-open way sounds great. But how does it work in practice? *Xtra Magazine.* https://xtramagazine.com/love-sex/relationships/gender-open-parenting-245816

Nolan, I. T., Kuhner, C. J., & Dy, G. W. (2019). Demographic and temporal trends in transgender identities and gender confirming surgery. *Translational Andrology and Urology, 8*(3), 184–190. https://doi.org/10.21037/tau.2019.04.09

Olson, K. R., Durwood, L., DeMeules, M., & McLaughlin, K. A. (2016). Mental health of transgender children who are supported in their identities. *Pediatrics, 137*(3). https://doi.org/10.1542/peds.2015-3223

Olson, K. R., Durwood, L., Horton, R., Gallagher, N. M., & Devor, A. (2022). Gender identity 5 years after social transition. *Pediatrics, 150*(2). https://doi.org/10.1542/peds.2021-056082

Ontario Human Rights Commission. (2014). *Policy on preventing discrimination because of gender identity and gender expression.* www.ohrc.on.ca/en/policy-preventing-discrimination-because-gender-identity-and-gender-expression

Orr, J. (2008, July 4). "Pregnant man" gives birth to baby girl. *The Guardian.* www.theguardian.com/world/2008/jul/04/usa.gender

Perlman, M. (2017, March 27). Stylebooks finally embrace the single "they." *Columbia Journalism Review.* www.cjr.org/language_corner/stylebooks-single-they-ap-chicago-gender-neutral.php

Pyne, J. (2016, November 22). Gender "pronoun war" is about freedom for sure, but not free speech. *NOW Toronto.* https://nowtoronto.com/news/gender-pronoun-war-free-speech

Rainbow Resource Centre. (2008). Two-Spirit people of the First Nations. Winnipeg, MB, Canada: Author. https://blogs.rrc.ca/diversity/wp-content/uploads/2014/12/TwoSpiritPeople.pdf

Reby, D., Levréro, F., Gustafsson, E., & Mathevon, N. (2016). Sex stereotypes influence adults' perception of babies' cries. *BMC Psychology, 4*(19). https://doi.org/10.1186/s40359-016-0123-6

Reis, E. (2016, September 25). Pronoun privilege. *The New York Times.* www.nytimes.com/2016/09/26/opinion/pronoun-privilege.html

Richards, J. (2015, February 18). Op-ed: It's time for trans lives to truly matter to us all. *The Advocate.* www.advocate.com/commentary/2015/02/18/op-ed-its-time-trans-lives-truly-matter-us-all

Scheim, A. I., Santos, H., Ciavarella, S., Vermilion, J., Arps, F. S. E., Adams, N., Nation, K., & Bauer, G. R. (2023). Intersecting inequalities in access to justice for trans and non-binary sex workers in Canada. *Sexuality Research and Social Policy, 20*(3), 1245–1257. https://doi.org/10.1007/s13178-023-00795-2

Serano, J. (2017, June 27). Debunking "trans women are not women" arguments. *Medium.* https://juliaserano.medium.com/debunking-trans-women-are-not-women-arguments-85fd5ab0e19c

Singh, A. A., Meng, S. E., & Hansen, A. W. (2014). "I am my own gender": Resilience strategies of trans youth. *Journal of Counseling & Development, 92*(2), 208–218. https://doi.org/10.1002/j.1556-6676.2014.00150.x

Sosin, K. (2023, March 23). *Most state bans on gender-affirming care for trans youth still allow controversial intersex surgery.* PBS NewsHour. www.pbs.org/newshour/health/most-state-bans-on-gender-affirming-care-for-trans-youth-still-allow-controversial-intersex-surgery

Statistics Canada. (2023, January 3). *Sex at birth and gender—2021 Census promotional material.* www.statcan.gc.ca/en/census/census-engagement/community-supporter/sex-birth-gender#

Steinmetz, K. (2016, January 8). This pronoun is the word of the year for 2015. *Time.* http://time.com/4173992/word-of-the-year-2015-they

Stryker, S. (2006). (De)subjugated knowledges: An introduction to transgender studies. In S. Stryker & S. Whittle (Eds.), *The Transgender Studies Reader* (pp. 1–17). Routledge.

Stryker, S. (2017). *Transgender history: The roots of today's revolution* (2nd ed.). Seal Press.

Tatum, A. K., Catalpa, J., Bradford, N. J., Kovic, A., & Berg, D. R. (2020). Examining identity development and transition differences among binary transgender and genderqueer nonbinary (GQNB) individuals. *Psychology of Sexual Orientation and Gender Diversity, 7*(4), 379–385. https://doi.org/10.1037/sgd0000377

Thorne, B. (1993). *Gender play: Girls and boys in school.* Rutgers University Press.

Walsh, B. (2015, December 4). The Post drops the "mike"—and the hyphen in "e-mail." *The Washington Post.* www.washingtonpost .com/opinions/the-post-drops-the-mike--and-the-hyphen-in-e-mail/ 2015/12/04/ccd6e33a-98fa-11e5-8917-653b65c809eb_story.html

Whitehead, J. (2018, March 14). Why I'm withdrawing from my Lambda Literary Award nomination. *Tia House: The Insurgent Architects' House for Creative Writing.* www.tiahouse.ca/joshua-whitehead-why-im-withdrawing-from-my-lambda-literary-award-nomination

Wiggins, C. (2022, November 1). Cis woman mistaken as transgender records being berated in bathroom. *The Advocate.* www.advocate.com/news/2022/11/01/ cis-woman-mistaken-transgender-records-being-berated-bathroom

Willsea, J. (2017, June 5). Please stop asking if my baby is a boy or a girl. *HuffPost.* www.huffpost.com/entry/please-stop-asking-if-my-baby-is-a-boy-or-a-girl_us_5935a65de4b0cfcda9169b3f

Wimalasundera, R. C., Trew, G., & Fisk, N. M. (2003). Reducing the incidence of twins and triplets. *Best Practice & Research: Clinical Obstetrics & Gynaecology, 17*(2), 309–329. https://doi.org/10.1016/ s1521-6934(02)00135-9

Woodward, A. (2023, April 6). At least 20 states ban trans women and girls from sports that match their gender. *The Independent.* www.independent.co.uk/news/world/americas/us-politics/transgender-athletes-ban-kansas-states-b2315626.html

Index

About the Author

Dr. Lee Airton (they/them) is an assistant professor of gender and sexuality studies in education at Queen's University. They were born and raised in Vancouver, lived for many years in Montreal, and now live in Kingston, Ontario, with their partner, cats, and too many tomato plants. Dr. Airton's research explores how Canadian K–12 education and teacher education are responding to gender identity and gender expression protections in human rights legislation. Dr. Airton has initiated campaigns and created resources that have informed the Canadian conversation about transgender people and gender diversity, such as TheyIsMyPronoun.com in 2012, the No Big Deal Campaign in 2016, and www.gegi.ca, a self-advocacy resource for K–12 students experiencing gender expression and gender identity discrimination at school, in 2020. In 2023, Dr. Airton and their colleagues released the document *No for Now: Guidance for School Staff on Supporting Transgender Students and Parent-Child Relationships* to inform policy and practice in schools across Canada and internationally (www.nofornow.ca). With Dr. Susan Woolley, Dr. Airton edited *Teaching about Gender Diversity: Teacher-Tested Lesson Plans for K–12 Classrooms*. Dr. Airton has been interviewed more than seventy times nationally and internationally on topics related to gender diversity. Learn more at LeeAirton.com.

Continue the Conversation and Share Your Learning!

Free and downloadable on GenderYourGuide.com: starting-place discussion guides that anyone can use to engage people around them in fostering gender-friendly spaces.

Each guide directs the user to selected passages from *Gender: Your Guide, 2nd Edition*, and includes meaningful prompts and questions to help a group bring the book's key takeaways to life. Each discussion guide is tailored to a particular context, purpose, or audience, including:

- Client Service
- K–12 Schools
- Colleges and Universities
- Workplaces
- Writers, Editors, and Journalists
- Gender-Neutral Pronoun Practice